ONWARD

May the joy,
move be toward
the head

Paul Off

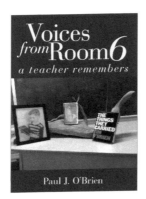

Voices from
Room 6

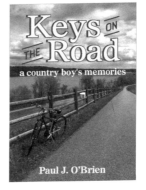

Keys on
the Road

CT
A Cat's Story

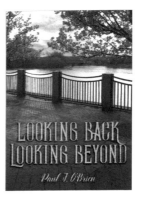

Looking Back
Looking Beyond

ONWARD

≫≫≫ *a collection of writings by* ≪≪≪

PAUL J. O'BRIEN

BOOK DESIGN BY The Troy Book Makers

Printed in the United States of America

The Troy Book Makers • Troy, New York • thetroybookmakers.com

To order additional copies of this title, contact your favorite local
bookstore or visit www.shoptbmbooks.com

ISBN: 978-1-61468-669-9

Contents

Dedication

The journey continues. Onward. We look for the light. In dark times, we discover that we can see in new ways. As I have done in my other books, I have continued to speak of experiences that enlightened me, often offering me new variations on life's meanings. I have also reached out to others, and they have shared their journeys too.

I thank the eight graduates, one from Notre Dame High School, and seven from Notre Dame-Bishop Gibbons School, who were magnanimous in spending time with me talking about the road they have traveled since high school: MaryAnne Panarese Vermillion, Jack Rightmyer, Larry Barry, Mark Koby, Kevin Barry, Rachel Rebanal Delgado, Imani Eichelberger, and Tina Jones.

I thank my wife Deborah for her constant source of strength and encouragement. She was always the first reader and editor of each piece. Invaluable. Much appreciation to my sister-in-law Elizabeth Cole for her careful editing and insightful comments. Carolyn Nadeau, my niece, helped me to think about the structure and how the many parts best work together.

A special note of appreciation to my friend Phyllis Budka who was the catalyst for my participation in the plays *The Claw* and "Anne of Green Gables Murders Everyone." I also thank Phyllis for giving me permission to quote from *The Claw* and to Union College Theater Director Randy Wyatt for permission to quote from "Anne of Green Gables Murders Everyone."

Thank you to my niece, Kathryn Nadeau, for the calligraphy. Thank you, Dan Pepe, for your words of wisdom, and much appreciation to Joseph Malinowski for your photography skills, giving the book its vital visual statement.

Preface

"In my end is my beginning."
— T. S. Eliot "East Coker" —

At the conclusion of this book, I speak in verse form about the past year and few months, the COVID time. All of the writing and a number of the experiences in this book took place during this viral time. It was a hard period, yet many of us found a way to "pivot" and make the best of it. Here in Niskayuna, we discovered inner reserves we didn't know we had, and we found that our patience could be stretched further than we knew. We read and we wrote and we shared home cooked meals, and yes, thank God, I was blessed with Debbie's genius in the kitchen. We discovered how creative and enterprising some of the museums and spiritual centers were, presenting webinars on Adirondack life, Emily Dickinson's flowers, and retreats that centered on prayer life.

Perhaps we were somewhat fortunate in having the situation that we did and the inner reserves and direction to draw from. For many, and we certainly felt this weight too, the times were dark, oppressive, and scary. We tried to follow as closely as we could the Governor's and CDC guidelines to protect ourselves and others, but when many others didn't, it created nerve-racking situations. We planned the shopping for food carefully and once in the store divided our list so that we could be as efficient as possible. All so-called common actions like dining out or getting a hair cut or attending Church services ground to a halt. And when our Church returned to the in-person Mass, it was carefully monitored, and we were wary and cautious. As a book-reading family, we faced challenges. The libraries were closed and once they finally resumed interacting with people, it was on-line, and all transactions were complicated and protracted in time.

What complicated life in addition to our response to the virus was an election year that both united and divided, adding to the horror of the George Floyd murder and its fallout across the country. The scales certainly tipped in the larger world to Dickens' "worst of times," and when 2021 began we were still doing that balance in our minds between hope (the vaccine) and doubt (our political and racial arenas).

Onward was written during this time. The title speaks of the movement in life that is always forward, with the memories and strength gleaned from the past as vital ingredients. A number of the pieces in the book have to do with theater: my trip to see *To Kill a Mockingbird* a few months before the pandemic; a short play I wrote about the contrast between then and now in high school students; three productions that I acted in — two live, and one virtual. I profiled eight graduates of Notre Dame-Bishop Gibbons; I had been with them in the classroom and now they shared the lives they had chosen — in a way, their stage.

The rest of the pieces, a few retrospectives both near and far, are reflections of where I am at this period of life and what matters to me. To cite again a quotation that means the world to me from "Little Gidding" in T. S. Eliot's *Four Quartets:*

> *"We shall not cease from exploration*
> *And the end of all our exploring*
> *Will be to arrive where we started*
> *And know the place for the first time."*

Yes, I'm still exploring.

Three Days

We all know the truth of the words, "What a difference a day makes." The events of one day can change the world. For most of us, however, days come and go without great consequences. And then there are those days at the end of which we feel joy at what we have experienced or those days when we give simple thanks that we made it through and will with God's grace return tomorrow for another day or, in some cases, we shake our heads in disbelief and express our relief that we survived the day. Here are three days that fit these categories.

Soaked

Soaked. I am standing outside the Marriott Marquis in Times Square, and I am soaked. If I had been a bit more of a trooper, I would have taken the subway up from Penn Station. "No, Deb, I'll just walk — it's only eight blocks or so," I told her as she dropped me off at the train station in Albany. "Thirty-fourth up to Forty-Sixth, more like twelve, Paul." I waved her off — "I'll be fine." Frankly, I don't have a lot of confidence in the subway, combined with my paranoia — did I see a knife sticking out of that guy's jacket — and I am, though slowing down, a walker. Still, I never figured that I would be absolutely drenched with sweat by the time I reached the Marquis. The navy blazer, in retrospect, was not a good idea, but the sun loved it.

"Deb," I say with some urgency on the cell, "I'm here at the Marquis, and I am drenched to the bone. I got Dan in thirty minutes. I can't go into his office like this."

"Ok, listen, you're in Times Square — there has to be a Gap or some store like that around. Just go in, buy a shirt, and change in the bathroom at the Marquis."

I scan the area, "Don't see any in sight, but I'll stroll around a bit. Can't believe it."

"Well, it is still August, and you did decide to walk the twelve blocks."

"I know, I should have taken a chance on the subway — maybe dodged a bullet."

"I know. Listen, you better hustle. You don't want to be late for Dan."

"You're right. Thanks for the idea. Talk later. Probably only a text though — going to get busy."

"I know. Be careful, Paul."

Before I move any farther into Times Square, it hits me — the Marquis Gift Shop. Grab a nice polo shirt there. That will save me time and a search.

Once you navigate the alphabetical logistics of the central elevator bank at the Marquis, it's a pretty cool ride up looking out through three glass walls. I get off at the eighth floor and head for the gift shop.

I can't believe it — no polo shirts, no dress shirts. Just tees with pictures of New York on them and sweat shirts, some with hoods — definitely not today. I let out a sigh and slip into a nearby bathroom. I look at myself in the mirror and try to pull the soaked shirt away from my body. What a mess. I glance at my watch — 1:55, and Dan is on at 2.

Dan, my nephew and godson, the four-year-old I carried on my shoulders in a race against Valerie, the eight-year-old Annandale, Virginia, street bully. Dan, who is now the GM of the Marriott Marquis. I'm on the elevator back down to the third floor, executive offices. He has told me where his office is on the third floor, and when I reach it, I ring a bell. A smiling woman comes to the door, opens it, and says, "You're Uncle Paul." I nod, and she directs me to a room to my right, where I see a sofa, a table, and a couple of chairs.

I set my bag, which holds a couple of books, a magazine, and a small umbrella, on the sofa to my right as Dan appears, big smile, and we share a warm combo hand-shake/hug. "How are you?" he says, sitting down on a chair to my right.

"Doing well," I say, wondering if he is noticing how soaked I am.

"Well, it's great to see you. Glad you made it to the City. You're going to like *Mockingbird*. Karen and I had a chance to see it a couple of months ago."

"Yes, really fortunate I got a chance to see the show — thank God for my friend Patti coming up with a ticket — otherwise, with the prices shooting up, no way would I have bought a ticket."

"Want to hear more about that, but first, ya got time for a little lunch?"

"Maybe something light — we have an early dinner scheduled before the play. But Dan, I've got a problem."

"What's that?"

"I'm a mess." And with those words, I pull open the right side of my jacket to show him my drenched shirt.

He looks at me, smiles, and says, "Follow me." He stands up, walks by me, and heads for the door. As we reach the elevator he says, "I have a small room here, which is great. I bicycle in, get here, grab a shower, and am ready for the day."

The room is on one of the guest room floors, and as we enter, there is a large closet to the left. Dan slides the door open, revealing about twenty shirts, dress and casual, followed by a number of suits. "Grab a shirt, freshen up — bathroom is right here," as he leans back and signals with his left hand, "relax a bit." He steps forward into a large combo living room-dining room space. "TV is here and there's a fridge back to the right. Help yourself to whatever you want. Soda, beer, snacks. When you are set, come on back down, and we can chat some more."

"Dan, you are a lifesaver."

He laughs and heads for the door, "See ya in a little while."

I take off my jacket and drape it over a dining room chair. In the closet, I see a light green polo shirt. "Perfect," I say. After taking off my shirt which I hang on the shower nozzle to dry out a bit, I do a thorough sponge bath, dry off, and then apply some of Dan's deodorant. I put on the polo shirt and sigh, "Thank you, Dan."

On the sofa, I send Debbie a text that all is well. I lean back and just think how lucky I am to have a nephew with a room at the Marquis who can solve my problem. I relax for a bit, then take my shirt, fold it up tightly and place it in the zippered compartment in the front of my shoulder bag. The jacket I don't put on but carry over my shoulder to dry out more — I am hoping Dan's deodorant can get the job done.

Back in the executive office, I hold on the lunch offer, but Dan and I have a good chat, with a lot of reminiscing. Though I know that he is very busy in his new position as GM, it's as if we are at the kitchen table in Raymertown, my childhood home, talking over an iced tea on a quiet summer day. Then I glance at my watch — almost 4. "Well, I guess I probably should be going. Meeting Patti, her husband and son, 4:30 at Daniela's."

"Heard of it," Dan says, "on Eighth. Well," he says as we both start to stand, "enjoy, and remember that when you and Deb come to the City, you have a place to stay here."

"That's great, Dan. I really appreciate it and want to let you know again, you saved me today!"

He laughs and says, "Anytime. Take care, Uncle Paul." Heading for the elevators, I reflect for a second on how well Dan has mastered the art of hospitality. I never once felt as if I was an inconvenience for him. He made me think that everything was just right.

For over a year, well for *Hamilton* it had been three years, there were two plays I had wanted to see — *Hamilton* and *To Kill a Mockingbird*. I had had one chance about a year prior when Debbie and I were staying for one night at the Marquis where she was at a conference. After we had checked in, we went for an afternoon walk and right nearby was the marquee for *Hamilton*. Debbie said, "Go see if there is a ticket."

"Really?"

"Sure, if there is one ticket, you can go tonight."

"Well, what are you going to do?"

"I'll hang in the room - we can get a bite to eat early."

Inside I saw movement in the ticket window. I approached, "Any chance you have a ticket available for tonight?"

"Let me check," the guy said. He fussed a bit among some papers and then said, "I have one ticket, in the next to last row in the mezzanine. One hundred and eighty dollars."

"Ok, I said, "I will be back in a minute if it's a go."

"They have one ticket for 180 bucks," I said to Debbie.

"Do it! You really want to see it! Go for it."

I hesitated, "What will you do tonight — really."

"I will be fine — do it!"

My mind flashed to what would be our evening if not for *Hamilton* - a nice dinner for two, usually with an Italian touch. "I can't do it," I said. "I would much rather have a nice, relaxing dinner with you. We don't get to the City that often, and that's what I want."

She stared at me, "You sure? You have your chance right now."

"No, it's dinner." I can see that another time.

And then *Hamilton* had finally come to Proctors Theater, and though it was dicey for a while because subscribers had the first shot, Debbie had gotten on the call-in number early the first day the non-subscriber tickets were available, and had secured us two tickets about twenty rows back from the stage. That production was now two weeks away. I knew the music — I had played the score from Hamilton numerous times, but now I would see it in three dimensions. I couldn't wait. On the other hand, I had not seized the opportunity early to get tickets for *Mockingbird* and then with Jeff Daniels giving some indication that his run as Atticus was nearing an end, prices had skyrocketed. No way — *Mockingbird* was out.

"Are you interested in seeing *To Kill a Mockingbird?*" my friend Patti asked.

"Are you serious?" I responded.

"Yes, we have four tickets, but Evan will be away at camp that week."

"My God, you sure? How much for the ticket?"

"No, we already have the tickets. No charge to you."

"I would absolutely love it," I said. "What's the date?"

"August 7th, 7 p.m."

"Perfect," I said, not even knowing whether there would be a conflict.

"You can ride down with us if you'd like."

My mind was already hopping and jumping — that would give me a chance to visit my nephew at the Marquis, his new work site. "That's ok, I'll grab the train, and meet you there. Wait, how about if I find us a restaurant and we meet for dinner?"

"I'd love that," Patti said, "Maybe in 4:30 - 4:45 range, not too far from the Shubert Theater.

"You got it," I said. "This is fantastic."

The rain had started, and I quickly popped on my nearly dry jacket and retrieved my umbrella. The city was rocking with its cacophony of horns, shouts, music, and the rushing and brushing of people. Standing under the canopy outside Daniela's were Patti, Gogi, and Ian. We said our hellos and then I glanced at my watch — 4:40. "I think we should go in." One thing I hadn't told Patti simply because I wanted to avoid any potential arguments was that I was paying for this dinner. They were treating me to a play I was longing to see; I would treat them to dinner.

Dinner was New York style — fast, efficient, servers not really smiling but courteous and workmanlike — with that look that says, "Glad you're here, but your time is about up." The restaurant had filled almost immediately, as we settled into our table near the front of the restaurant. We had good dinner conversation about being in the city, and it was exciting to see how thrilled Ian was at the chance to see the play. I don't remember what the others had, but I do remember that I enjoyed my Pasta Bolognese and a glass of chianti — maybe it was two. And then I began to think of making my move to take care of the bill. The signal came when Patti asked Gogi if he wanted to do dessert, and he said, "Why don't we wait and have dessert and coffee later." She said fine. That was my signal that their ordering was over. Time for my move.

"Don't you dare!" Patti said, gripping my arm as I started to stand up.

"I'm just going to the bathroom," I said.

"I know you," she said. "You are not paying for this dinner."

I slouched back, "Why?" I said.

"No questions. This is our treat."

"Well," I said, "In that case, I don't need the bathroom."

She laughed, "I thought you might try something."

I had one other problem I hadn't yet shared with Patti. I am claustrophobic, and theater seating can really scare me with its tightness. I think on the way over or in the lobby of the theater I asked Patti if I could sit in the seat closest to the aisle. She said sure, that was fine.

The seats were very tight, not much body room, with little space in front for the knees — I was the third seat in. For a moment, I thought there was hope, but when I looked at the crowd filling the theater, I knew there was no chance that the two seats to my left would remain empty. And within seconds they were filled. Panic was rising quickly —and for a few seconds, I thought of telling Patti I might have to get up and see if I could work out a deal with the usher to allow me to stand in the back. Then Gogi said something that made Ian laugh and for a second my mind relaxed. It was almost curtain time — if I could hang on, there was hope.

In front of what appeared to be the side of a weathered red barn serving as the stage curtain, two characters emerged — a grown-up Scout and Jem — and we heard Scout's words, "Something didn't make sense," as she spoke about the reports that Bob Ewell died instantly when he fell on his knife. And then the wall rose and we were in the play.

My claustrophobia was eclipsed by the vivid and compelling story that appeared before my eyes. Certain images and moments remain with me: Atticus searching, trying to find a way to reach the heart of the people in Maycomb; Calpurnia speaking in ways that the Lee text never did, challenging Atticus's view that one should respect everyone; the judge responding to the prosecutor's questioning of the legitimacy of Tom Robinson's swearing in because of his withered hand with the statement, "I can't believe you said that!" And then ten minutes later in the trial, the judge slamming his gavel down and saying again, "I can't believe you said that." Tom, a pillar of a wronged person yet with a dignity rising above the others — his first words to Atticus before the trial begins, "I was guilty as soon as I was accused." Atticus's closing speech — in its own way as powerful as Gregory Peck's — "In the name of God, just let him go home." Bob Ewell, confronting Atticus with his vile and ugly comments after Tom Robinson has been shot and killed; and Atticus walking slowly off the porch and right up to Ewell who continued to spew his racist comments, Atticus saying that Bob knew what the real problem was — no one in the courtroom believed him but they were too afraid to speak the truth; then when Bob continued, Atticus, to my utter amazement, making a jujitsu move putting Bob in some type of an armlock, telling him that he better not say another word. I wanted to stand up and applaud — Atticus was doing what I always wanted him to do. And then the play closes with Scout and Jem having the final words as this heart-breaking period from their past closes.

It was one of those nights that will remain in my mind. All thanks to the generosity of my good friend. Almost in a trance, we moved slowly up a few steps and then down the almost hushed stairs, stepping out onto a very busy street, like stepping out of a dream. Patti asked me if I had time for dessert, but I had a 10:50 train, and it was already nearing ten. "Thanks a million," I said, giving Patti a hug and shaking hands with Gogi and Ian.

As I reached the corner I had a panic that is not uncommon for me in New York City — was I heading in the right direction? I stopped at a pretzel cart and asked, "If I turn here and start down Seventh and stay on it, I will reach Penn Station, correct?" He looked at me, smiled, and said, "Yes, but that's a hell of a walk. Grab the subway - it's a lot easier." I glanced at my watch — just after ten. "Thanks, I'll be fine."

Twelve blocks, I said to myself, I better kick butt. I had the full flavor of New York at night on the way down. People handing me night club brochures, others asking for a handout, some on the sidewalk asleep, at one point a couple in each other's arms — asleep on the sidewalk. It was about 10:40 when I entered Penn Station. I approached the area that always seems like a guessing game — which track will I be on tonight? Thank God, I saw the Albany, Track 6 sign!

The trip home would be a treat because Debbie had reserved for me a seat in Business, First Class, plenty of room if I needed to take a snooze. I entered the car and flopped down in a seat.

Once again the shirt I was wearing, Danny's shirt, was soaked. But now it was all ok. Debbie would understand. And as the train began to roll north into the night, I put my head back and one haunting line from my day returned, "In the name of God, just let him go home."

Twenty Four Hours in the Life of a Retired Teacher

Monday, January 4th, 2021

I am a night owl and rarely go to bed before midnight. It is just past mid-night as I descend the stairs, Casey racing ahead of me to get his night-time food snack. Sunday had been a whirlwind of emotions: after watching the Giants squeak by the Dallas Cowboys in the afternoon, thus keeping them on the edge of the playoffs, my spirits were hopeful. Alas, the Eagles playing a lackluster game were unable to beat the team the Giants needed to have them beat — the Washington Football team. Until the fourth quarter, there had been a semblance of hope, but then the Eagles seemed to throw in the towel, and Washington wrapped the game up.

I am a news junkie and decided postgame to check MSN-BC, but it was not a good move — the discussion was about President Trump's call to the Georgia Secretary of State and Trump's effort to cajole the secretary into securing him enough votes to make him a winner in Georgia. I stayed with that discussion longer than I should have. So now I'm in the kitchen, getting Casey some canned food and a teaspoon of dry food. Whenever I lean down with his food, his back arches way up — can't explain the move — but I assume it is the verbal equivalent of "Oh, goodie, finally."

I step out into the small dining room and glance to my left — my desk lights are still on in the back room. Entering the back room, I see snow falling gently and then check to see that the gas stove is set at 58 degrees. In front of the desk to the right, Casey's "window" is cranked open about an inch and the temp drops a few degrees as I approach — Debbie knows that he loves the little opening to the outside world of birds, chipmunks, squirrels, and stray cats. I lock the window — I would even if it were summer. I have always been obsessed about safety, though I must say that I have never felt safer in any house or living space than I have here in Niskayuna.

Even at the Wade Lupe Towers in our fifth floor apartment, I never ruled out the idea that intruders, invaders, burglars, kidnappers, could lower themselves from the roof or repel off the side of the building and come in through the bedroom windows — dramatically or like the coolest sleuths. One morning about seven I thought it had happened — a shotgun blast shattering glass in the front room. I should have grabbed my small baseball bat under the bed, but because it was daylight, I had more nerve and simply raced out into the living room. The floor was littered with glass and near my reading chair was a golf ball. When I picked it up, I saw the logo — Marriott Hotels. Ironic because I have a few relatives who work for Marriott. And then of course it all fell into perspective — the Wade Lupe Towers was adjacent to the twelfth hole of the Stadium Golf Course. Now to put it into another perspective, that tee shot was horrific. It might have set a local record for the worst slice of the summer.

I looked at Deb and said, "I'll be right back" and I raced out our door and up the stairway to the roof that overlooked the twelfth green. Three guys were approaching the green, and I heard a few "Geeess" and "Oh my Gods." I chose not to say anything or try to throw the ball down which I still held in my hand. I think I could have reached the green, and now that I think of it, that would have been pretty funny: the errant slice returns to the green, with maybe a few words like "Did you lose this?" Or "About a one putt from there." But I didn't — I watched them putt out and then returned down the stairs to our apartment.

In the reflection of the back room windows, I see the lights of our Christmas angel in front of the house. Before sitting down at the desk for a final few minutes, I walk out to the front room and decide to take a pic of the angel. As I look at it through my cell phone, I see the lamp next to Debbie's chair reflected to the left off the angel. I take the pic and decide to post it on FB.

Of course, I'm on FB now and check for any late messages and then I wish Happy Birthday to my FB friends whose birthday falls on Jan. 4th. There is one request for donations on a birthday, but I decided a while back that I can't get into that — with over 2500 friends, mostly students I have taught, I get about one request for a cause every other day. I see that my Words with Friends partners (right now five players, though I am trying to cut back) have all added a word, and so I take my time to play a word that gives me points and doesn't leave too much of an opening for an easy triple word score. On Messenger, I send out a few fun emoji to those who have a good sense of humor, express condolences to someone whose cat is nearing the end, and get an update on the world of California from two different friends living out there. One, Patti, has sent me a clever video of a park's Christmas light display, not a trace of snow. It is after 12:30 — time to head to bed. In the hallway, I turn the heat down to 60 degrees. In the bed, Debbie, turned towards the far wall, has been asleep for three hours, and Casey has curled up and nestled in along her legs. I notice on the chair holding the clean laundry are the pjs I wore last night — usually I get two days out of them, but Debbie has been especially assiduous during the COVID period with the laundry.

As I ease into bed — ease is a word I like to use — Casey opens his eyes, looks at me, stretches just a bit, and yawns. He nestles back as I set up my charging device for my iPhone, make sure there is enough distilled water for my C-Pap, and then settle back into my four pillows, still sitting up for the most part — reading time. I pick from the pile of books next to my bed the novel *On Earth We're Briefly Gorgeous* by Ocean Vuong, a young Vietnamese writer, known more for his poetic skills, evident also in his fiction. The book is compelling, haunting, and beautiful with a Vietnamese narrator who addresses his mother as he tries to find coherence in their lives. I finish a section in which the Mom has managed to convey the story to the narrator, her son, about an older child she aborted. The chapter ends with a full sense of her emptiness and her regret. I glance at my watch — 1:20 a.m., time to sleep. I set the book down, rig up my C-Pap, shut off the light and then fall back into my pillows, sliding them around until I find a comfort zone. I reach back with my left hand, tap Debbie twice while saying "good night," and then touch Casey. Okay, Sleep, let's go.

My dream is from the far reaches — seems like a river in Colorado or something, and I have been swimming or just floating along when I almost bump into what I first think is a floating limb, which upon closer inspection I realize is a alligator floating along the shore — I turn and swim away slowly. I keep looking and there appears to be something wrong with the alligator. Back on shore I look carefully — it is moving slightly but seems sick or injured. At that moment, a local conservation guide strolls by, and he tells me that I better take the alligator with me. I can't believe it — and feel totally discombobulated, and then he says, "Come on, I'll help you load him in your car." I protest but to no avail. And then the two of us are lugging the gator who is "still alive" to my car which happens to be a hatchback. We set the gator down, and I open the back up. We then shove the gator in — I have the tail part and have to twist him a bit so that he fits. "That will do it!" the guide says, "Good luck."

Something is standing on my body, and I hear Debbie's voice from the doorway, "Come on Casey, time for breakfast." He launches off the bed from my body, and she pulls the door shut so that I can sleep a bit longer. I lift myself up and look around the room, just in case a gator slipped in, then I fall back. As I lie in bed half asleep, I hear a snowplow speed by, and I wonder how much snow we have gotten. In days of old, I would have gotten up two or three times in the night to see if a school snow day was possible — now retired and with COVID at its peak, the world has changed and snow days seem to be a thing of the past. The heat kicks on, and the house seems to be ready to launch itself. The plow goes by again, having turned around at the end of the block. Something about the sound of the plow tells me that there isn't a lot of snow. Thumping and more thumping in the hallway as Casey races by the bedroom door chasing one of the balls Debbie has thrown.

Time for some foot exercises in bed. I slide out from under the covers, lift my left leg and rotate my left foot ten times clockwise and then ten times counter clockwise; then

I repeat and drop the left foot. I do the same with my right foot. This exercise routine is my first effort of the day to try to deal with the neuropathy that has taken over my brother and confined him to a walker and his indoor scooter. He has me by quite a few years, and I hope I can fend it off for a while with exercise. Time to get up, and I roll out.

After the bathroom, I stroll down our short hallway, usually singing a nonsense song. Today's is, "How are the little pippers today, I hope they're not feeling grey — that's not the wayyyyy — for my little pippers."

And then I hear Debbie say, "Casey, guess who's up? You know what that means, Casey." And already Casey has moved from the backroom and is headed toward the kitchen. I step out into the back room and am stunned at how the snow has created a backyard winter wonderland. "Lovely," I say.

Debbie is off to the far right on the sofa, immersed in her books and her Kindle, the fire in the gas stove creating a cozy environment for reading.

"Very pretty, " she says, looking outward.

"Yes, I probably should get the snowblower out even though it looks like only a few inches."

"Good idea — last time you didn't and it kind of froze over."

"Yeah, Charlie" — the name I gave my snowblower — "had a day off. I'll have to fire him up today. I'm gonna eat first."

"Sure."

I enter the kitchen, and Casey is standing near his food dish and whining - not really a meow, more of a half cry of a poor little starving cat. I add to his agita by saying, "Oh, you sad, starving thing — no one ever feeds you. More, you say, More. We are so cruel to our little Casey." I pick up his food dish, add a teaspoon full of canned food, and place it on the floor. He looks at me for a second as if to say, "Is this a trick?" And then he dips his head to dine.

On the counter is my cup which holds a strainer with tea Debbie has left for me. She has a variety of teas and usually creates a blend. Since I have been retired — six years — tea has become my morning drink, rather than the Stewarts' coffee I used to stop and pick up each morning, along with the *Post* and the *Daily News*, on the way to school. I put some water into the electric water pot and click it on. On the cutting board are half an apple, half an orange, and a plastic container of blueberries. I eat the apple over the sink and then slice the half orange into four. I also eat those over the sink and flip the rinds into the disposal with the remains of the apple. The water boils in the pot, but before I add the water, I take the swirly honey stick, dip it into a jar of honey, and place the stick over the tea in the strainer. Then I pour the hot water over the honey and tea, turning the honey stick to get it all into the tea water. Done. While waiting for about two minutes, I grab a bowl, put in some of Debbie's crunchy cereal that she keeps in a jar, add some blueberries, take the stick from the tea, wash it, dip for more honey and then let it drip on the cereal. Wash the stick quickly, grab some soy milk from the fridge, and add to the cereal — and I am ready for the second part of my breakfast. I place the tea on the stand next to the sofa and the cereal on the sofa's arm — a bit dangerous but hey, I just drove away from a river with an alligator in my car! One more thing before I dine. I open the garage door and see the blue bag with the *Times* in it and the orange bag with the *Gazette* in it resting on the newly fallen snow in the driveway. I am in my pjs, and my hoodie, with my slippers on, but I can shake off any snow when I get back inside. It is about three inches with about 10 inches at the bottom of the driveway where the snow plow has pushed up the street snow.

Back on the sofa, my ritual begins with the *Gazette*. Usually a quick look at the sports — a recurring pattern since

I first started looking at the sports section of the *Troy Record* while eating breakfast at the age of eight or so. Then the front section with the headlines, and I must admit, the next thing is the obituary page, which echoes what my father used to look at first as he got older and older. I am finding more and more familiar faces, one reason might be the fact that I taught high school for forty seven years, and got to know a lot of people in the area. Then it's the local section, at the end of which is the editorial page, columns, and letters. The last few months have been a real grind politically, and I can often come away from this section depressed.

"Don't forget you need to do your poem this morning," Debbie says on the way to the kitchen.

"Thanks for reminding me," I say. On Saturday, she and I had participated in a Zoom retreat from the Campion Center in Weston, MA. The theme was "Poems of Joy: Savoring the Gifts of Incarnation." The retreat had been excellent, and we had been given a wonderful handout of poetry and readings. Our task to be completed and sent in by Monday was to write a poem in response to a painting we had been given called "Madonna and Child."

"I will do it right after the snow blowing."

Before a quick look at the *Times*, which I usually save until later in the morning or early afternoon, I pick up my fully-charged lap top and check out Facebook. I look to see if I need to make any moves in the Word Game, look at any postings to me or responses to the picture I took late last night of our front yard angel with its light snow cover. Then I usually decide to post something maybe inspirational or humorous or thought-provoking. I check out my poetry websites, "Poem a Day" and "Writer's Almanac" and since I'm not moved by today's entry, decide to do a little dialogue with Charlie, the snow blower. First I must go out to the garage and take of pic of Charlie with the open garage door behind him revealing the task ahead. I take my pic and come back in to write my dialogue — my chat with Charlie as we prepare for the morning task. I must admit that I chuckle to myself while doing it. I then post the pic with the dialogue, hoping that someone else might find a little humor here.

Okay, the fun is over. "Get to work, Paul." I am a little bit like "Brer Rabbit in the Briar Patch" with some jobs. I like snow blowing because you can see the clear results of your work, and I love seeing how the shoot of snow creates mounds in our yard and the neighbor's yard. After some resistance before the first storm — Yikes - 33 inches — Charlie has been great, firing up on the first yank of the cord. I navigate around our Subaru and create enough space for Debbie to move it so that I can do the space it was in, mostly snow that has fallen off the car. Debbie meanwhile has done the sidewalk. I am pretty much done with our driveway and decide to just clean the entrance of the neighbor's driveway across the street. After creating a pretty good space, I look over at Debbie who gives me a visual signal — sort of thumb across the throat which says, "That's enough! We don't want a heart attack here."

Back inside I decide to return to my dialogue with Charlie and give him some praise for a good job. Charlie is frustrated at something today, but his mood changes dramatically after the praise, and the scene ends with him winking at me twice. I post on Facebook. I tend to get a range of responses in the 25 - 30 people who check in: Some say, "Has the Pandemic driven you off the edge?" while others say, "You should write a children's story about a snow blower named Charlie."

Debbie tells me that the Open Door called and my book is in. I have ordered three, but I think this one is *The Book Woman of Troublesome Creek,* having been highly recommended by a former student, now a teacher, the week before.

Anna at the Open Door front desk had told me that this one was the most readily available.

"Great," I say to Debbie, thinking of my Christmas gift cards.

"And my book is ready at the library for pickup at 1:30."

"Cool." I say. "We can grab your book and then head down to the Door. Maybe after a light lunch?"

To the poem: I am now in the back room at my desk, Casey on a blue blanket two feet away on the desk, staring out at a large squirrel on the table of artificial geraniums we place there for winter decorations. Now to the task we had been assigned on our Saturday retreat. The picture is of a Black Madonna seated holding a baby in swaddling clothes. Strength and determination radiate from her face as she looks off to her left. There is a halo effect over her head and then a crown design and behind that a grey-draped curtain. To her left are sharp geometric patterns and curled designs, creating a spatial tension. On the floor behind her appears a weasel, and to the right, above and behind are warlike masks and vehicles. There are four butterflies, two on each side of her that seem to be admiring the Madonna and Child. When I look at the painting, I see two things primarily: the woman's strength and the world she is surrounded by — and all I can think of is "Guernica."

I recall Picasso's "Guernica" in the Prado when I had the chance to see his masterpiece on a school trip: its focus the aftermath of the bombing of the town of Guernica in images of brutality and suffering. The reality that Picasso portrays is of the nightmarish world of humankind. The painting I am now looking at seems to incorporate that surrounding darkness. The woman's face in the painting grows stronger, and it is with her that I center my poem. I spend about thirty minutes and arrive at what I think is something worthy of sending to the retreat center.

MADONNA AND CHILD

In the center of the world
That rings of Picasso's "Guernica"
A woman of strength and determination
Lifts her head in thought
Resolute
Proud
She knows that she holds in her arms
A Child of Peace
A Child of Hope
A Child of Love
So absolutely crucial
In a world of darkness, suffering
and blindness.

With unwavering grit
She steels herself
She will hold
and she will guide
This Child
Until He stands
and begins
His journey
to change
Our World
With Peace
And Hope
And Love.

Debbie finished her poem a while ago, and we gather in her study to share each other's creation. Hers is denser and gives more attention to the Afrocentrism of the painting — I like it, and I am pleased that we have both celebrated the woman's strength.

"Ok, good, I will email these to Father John. But wait," — I have started out of the room — "we should have a little lunch before we head out to the library and bookstore," she says.

"Soup," I say.

"Sure, what kind?"

"Since we had tomato last time, let's do chicken noodle."

"That's good," she says. "I'll be out in a minute and put out some stuff." Now the secret, which she really knows, is that I am not really much of a chicken fan, as a matter of fact, I could easily be a vegetarian, but I still like an occasional burger, meat balls on pasta, and maybe roast chicken if it is roasted for about five hours.

I open the can of Progresso Chicken Noodle and pour the contents into a small pot on the stove. I turn the burner on to 6 — don't like it to get too hot too fast. Debbie arrives and puts out some breads — rye, six grain, and pita, some veggies — carrots and celery, which she cuts into bite size bits, a container of hummus, a plastic tray of spinach, some potato chips, and a jar of peanut butter. I had planned to have one slice of six grain with peanut butter, but I change my mind and take a piece of pita, cut it in half, spread some hummus inside and then add a few leaves of spinach. To my plate I add five or six celery and carrot pieces, and a small handful of potato chips, forty percent less fat. The soup is beginning to bubble, and I turn the burner down to one. I grab two bowls out of the cupboard and place them on the counter. I then ladle soup into my bowl, being careful to just get broth and noodles. "Make sure I get one or two noodles with my chicken," Debbie says from behind me. I smile, finish ladling, and add some pepper.

One more touch, "Diet Coke?" I ask. She says, "Sure," and I retrieve two small cans from the fridge. I stick the unopened Coke into the pocket of my hoodie, grab my plate, and soup, and head for my favorite spot on the sofa in the front room. I place the soup and the plate on the arm of the sofa, danger-ous location again, the soda on the stand back to the left. I sit down, and now is when I pick up the *New York Times* which is on the sofa to my right.

I skim some front page stories on the action coming up on Wednesday with the Vice-President who will preside over the official count of electoral votes for the Presidency, in the past largely a formality, but this year due to challenges from Ted Cruz, Josh Hawley, and a few others the day will be pro-tracted. Casey jumps up on the sofa to my right and is eye-ing my nearly empty bowl of soup. "No, Casey, this is people food. You have had yours." He looks at me as if I have spoken Russian. "No," I say more firmly following Debbie's frequent directive — "You have to give him a firm NO!" I think he is now reading my mind because he turns and jumps down.

I take a quick look at the op-ed page and see a column entitled, "Vaccines are Safe, No Matter What Robert Kenne-dy, Jr. Says." The article has been written by his niece Kerry Kennedy Meltzer, who is a physician at New York-Presby-terian Medical Center. The highlighted line that catches my attention is "I love my uncle. But when it comes to vaccines, he is wrong." There are many reasons why this article draws me: I was a huge fan of Bobby Kennedy, Robert's dad, I have family members who are very interested in this debate — vaccination vs anti-vaccination, and I am preparing to get the COVID 19 vaccination when it is available.

I munch away on my sandwich and side goodies as I read the article, siding with Kerry because of the principal influences in my life being pro-vaccine and knowing how crucial it is for enough people to get the vaccine in order for it to be effective against the virus. I finish the article and decide to forward it to my brother who is a physician and already has had the shot and my sister who is a nurse and who would be interested in hearing this opinion.

"Any cookies left?" I ask Debbie.

"I think there are two," she says. "I'll have one too. And then we better think about getting underway. I don't want to be late for the library book."

I almost continue straight down Union Street, when Debbie says, "What are you doing?" It hits me that the book is not downtown but at the Niskayuna Branch. The pandemic has changed the world of libraries in many ways, one is the way a take-out book is done. It begins with your search on the library website for the book you desire. Once you find it, you place a request on line. The response will indicate where you are on the waitlist for the book and when it should be available. You wait until you receive an email from the library that the book is available. Then you call the library and arrange a pick-up time for the book. When you get there, you follow all the COVID-19 protocols: wear a mask, social distance, etc.

I drive by the entrance to the library, and Debbie gets out by the side entrance walkway. I make the loop in the circular drive and have to navigate among others who are here for pickups. From my vantage point there is one person ahead of her on the walkway, and then a person emerges, and the one ahead of her enters. She stands alone. A minute or so and the person exits, and Debbie standing back enters. Once inside, she will see a table divided with a plexiglass. She has to show her library card, which is compared to the number they have in their file. Then the librarian takes Debbie's book and slides it through the opening in the plexiglass. The book is *The Sicilian Method* by Andrea Camilleri. The only reason I know about this whole process is that she has told me. I have not done it once.

The Open Door Bookstore has become almost a second home for me. I always find the place warm and inviting with its combination of book store and gift shop, and since I have gotten into the world of writing, I have found Janet Hutchinson, the owner, and her staff lovely and easy to work with. They have gone out of their way to make each book signing an excellent experience, even during the pandemic when they set up a table just outside the store where I could greet people and autograph books.

Today is an especially good day for me because I have two fifty dollar Christmas gift cards from the Open Door and one of their discount coupons you earn once you spend a hundred dollars or so. "Hi, Paul," Anna, an ebullient spirit, says from the check-out counter to the left of the entrance. "Hey, Anna," how you doing?" She nods, smiles, and says, "Doing ok."

My brother sent me a book for Christmas but to Debbie, a check to buy a book. She knows the book she wants and has headed to the nature shelves. While I head to the fiction section to the left of check-out, I ask Anna if she is holding a book for me. She looks behind her at the two shelves of books ordered and finds my name. "*The Book Woman of Troublesome Creek,*" she says, holding up the book. "This sounds very interesting."

"A friend recommended it" — a former student who teaches in a middle school and who had invited me to read my story of our three legged cat to her class last year. "Her mom gave it to her, and she loves it. You can just set it there.

I'll grab it when I get some other stuff." I see a new collection of short stories on the fiction shelf that I had read good things about, and I take that one. To my left is the best sellers and down a bit the poetry section. I select *Best Poems of 2020* for one of the teachers at ND-BG with whom I exchange gifts. I then move past the check-out counter and into the children's section, looking for a book called *Sparky,* a children's story that Debbie had me read, the story of a pet sloth that I loved. No luck — we may order that one on Amazon because we want to ship a copy to our nephew who loves sloths and had them as pets.

Debbie comes down the aisle and hands me the book she has chosen — *What It's Like To Be a Bird*, a new best-selling book about birds. The cover alone of the oversized book tells me that it is going to have wonderful illustrations. "Add this to your collection," she says. "I'm all set — I'm just going to look around some more."

I need another small item for another teacher at ND-BG, and I see a small trivia game called "Inspirational Women." Perfect, I think, this teacher is a strong woman, and I think could have some fun with this in her class. I swing around and walk to the far side past the discount books and up to the calendars where I pick up a desk calendar entitled *Dreyer's English* based on a book of style and usage that I own.

One more stop, and I am all set for today. My favorite section in the gift side of the store: the tiny glass animals that I give as small presents. I may be the best purchaser the Open Door has of these tiny glass animals. Over the last fifteen to twenty years, I have purchased hundreds, giving them as small gifts for graduations, birthdays, and just for serendipitous moments. Once I was looking for a unicorn to give one of our English teachers who taught *The Glass Menagerie* in the spring each year. Alas, there were none. And

Lynnea who usually works the gift side of the store brought out from behind the desk four or five bags of little glass animals — we must have looked at two hundred searching for a unicorn. And when there was no hope, I said, "If you ever get one in, call me." About a year and half later, she called one afternoon, and said, "Guess what!" I said "I have no idea," and she responded, "A unicorn came in."

"Hi there," I say to Courtney who is working in the gift section today, "mind if I set my stuff here while I check the little creatures?"

She nods and says, "I just put a few new ones out."

Right now, I have a few in my desk at home, but I want to take a look just to see if there are any exciting new ones. I am not disappointed: a multi-colored rooster, almost a dandy, jumps out at me, and I reach down and gently pick him up. "Found one."

The bill totals in the $180 range, but after my two gift cards and the Open Door discount, I owe 67 dollars and change. The bag is heavy, but it is a good heavy, and it's a nice feeling to support a store that is so good to you. Debbie is chatting with Anna as I emerge from the gift side, and Anna says, "Looks as if you have some reading ahead."

"Nothing like it," I say as we prepare to return to the world.

It is pushing three and I check to see if Debbie wants to be tempted with one of our favorite road treats. "Hot chocolate and split a Cruller or just a hot chocolate?"

"Maybe a hot chocolate, but let's hold the Cruller, unless you want one. I've got a pretty good dinner planned —don't want to eat too much."

Turns out to be a bit disappointing — the hot chocolate is watered down, it's hot all right, but pretty weak in the chocolate department. "That seems to happen about every third time," Debbie says. "You think the hot chocolate machine gets tired out?"

"Exhausted," I say.

Home, and, of course, that means attention to the little guy — Casey. As we enter, he usually rolls over and stretches, which is a signal for a rub, and "I am ready for food." I let Debbie handle the food — she is determined to keep Casey in the 9 pound range — ten being for her a danger zone. I don't consider that too much of a worry right now: he has such explosive energy and often races through the house from one window to another looking for whatever little animals are nearby, and when he plays with his little toys, he engages with great vigor.

"I'm going to hit the bike," I say, knowing that she will be heading out for her afternoon walk shortly, usually about an hour walk in the neighborhood. She loves to walk, the only negative being the dogs she encounters that seem very aggressive behind invisible fences and those that are on leashes but seem almost as if they could yank the leash right out of their owner's hands with ease. One afternoon after she had gone out, I noticed an elderly gentleman walk by with a young German Shepherd challenging the leash, and they were heading down the street that Debbie often returns on. On the way to the car, I spotted my hammer and flipped it on the front seat just in case. I drove down the street but did not see the man or Debbie. I circled the area for a bit and then drove home. She was there — had returned another way — but she was pleased to hear that I had worried enough to set out to rescue her if she was in trouble.

I have knees that are getting worse each day and now I don't do well with walking, but I can do the stationary bike, which is upstairs in our small television/library/dining/exercise room. I usually have four or five books with me — and like to keep all of them going. Today I carry up along with my water the following books: *On Earth We're Briefly Gorgeous*, a novel by Ocean Vuong; *The Liar's Club*, a memoir by Mary Karr —- a book which I have already finished years ago, but I am rereading the early chapters to study her technique; *Reading Like a Writer*, a non-fiction book on writing for those who love to read, by Francine Prose; *Daddy*, the collection of short stories, by Emma Cline, I bought today; and *Grammar for a Full Life*, a book I recently ordered from Amazon about a new approach to grammar, by Lawrence Weinstein.

I place the books on a food tray next to the bike along with the television remote and my water. I remove my Fitbit from my left wrist and place it in my left pants pocket to keep track of the "steps" I will record: usually an hour on the bike with an average of somewhere between 20-25 miles an hour translates into 4000 steps. I turn the television on to CNN with Anchor Jake Tapper, whom I like, and put him on mute. I try to focus on the reading, and look up occasionally to see who his guests are and scan the headlines across the bottom of the screen.

I open with Prose's book because I can read a section that is complete in itself. Today, I pick up on the chapter entitled "Sentences," an exploration of the art and care that writers use to construct sentences. One of the sentences she explores is from Samuel Johnson's *The Life of Savage*. The sentence is 134 words long, but Prose points out that its most striking quality is its clarity, even with its ten commas and three semi-colons. I read more and decide to stop at the point where Prose is about to examine the opening sentence of the Virginia Woolf essay, "On Being Ill." I set it down and pick up Karr's book. I find an almost immediate link with my own past when I read her memories of her Dad, especially the sense details associated with a trunk her father had left at the house: "I can still smell the odor that came out of the trunk when we crowbarred the padlock off and opened it. The smell had seeped into the letters and endures there — damp paper, and gun oil, and chalk from the edges of a puzzling cedar box, which we eventually figured out was a turkey call" (pg. 19). I slow down the peddling and let her book close in my hand, as I am transported back to my father's truck — sitting in it after his work day on the state highway: cigar aroma in the cab, on the seat to the right, the fragments of extra sharp cheese from Starkzie's in Center Brunswick, and the sweet, intoxicating smells of the nearly empty can of beer on the floor still containing a few drops which slide smoothly down my throat. Back peddling, I read a few pages more of Karr, and then pick up Vuong's novel. I love the title "On Earth We're Briefly Gorgeous" — what a poetic way to capture the ephemeralness of life. I am reading a chapter about the narrator being drawn into an emotional relationship with an older boy when I glance up for a second and see Daniel Pearl's face on CNN.

In a flash I set the book down and hit the unmute button on the remote. It is now Chris Christie talking to Jake Tapper about Daniel's murder and how he wants the alleged killer of Pearl, Ahmed Omar Sheikh, brought to justice here in the United States. Sheikh, a Pakistani, had been sentenced to death for the abduction and murder of Pearl, but the murder conviction was overturned and he had been released. Pearl, a *Wall Street Journal* reporter, had special meaning for me because we had studied his work in Pop Culture class, and I had shown the class the documentary of his life and death. I had also shared with the class moments from the memoir entitled *A Mighty Heart* written by his wife, Mariane Pearl.

I mute the button and finish the chapter in Vuong's book. Heading toward five, maybe a few minutes with the grammar book by Weinstein. The epigraph for the "Introduction" is one of my favorite quotations: "The limits of my language mean the limits of my world" — Ludwig Wittgenstein. The thesis seems to be something along the line of a correlation between well-being and the choices we make in our writing. The chapters are relatively short — it's closing in on five, and my snoozer awaits, but I decide to zip through the first chapter entitled "Getting Noticed." The chapter is about colons and their use. He argues that sometimes we need to take a stand, assert ourselves and he cites the biologist Lewis Thomas thoughts about the colon, those two vertically arranged dots, "Listen up, please, here's what you should know..." (pg 11). They call attention to what is to follow. He cites his father who used to say, "Don't let people walk all over you" (pg. 13). And then points out how often his father would insert colons in his writing. Weinstein concludes the first chapter with Martin Luther King's use of a colon in closing his great "I Have a Dream" speech. This colon signaled a pause and told his audience to listen carefully to what was coming, and then he contrasts that colon signal with the sentence without the colon. Hmmmmm, Weinstein does have me thinking and making me want to read more of this book. I close the book and look up to see Wolf Blitzer's face on the screen. Time for a snoozer.

Covered with a red woolen throw blanket, I drift off in the bedroom within minutes with the television on low — the news is at this point white noise. And I know it's a fairly deep sleep because when Debbie wakes me usually shortly after six, I am often totally disorientated: "What day is it?" "How long was I asleep?" "Is it dinner time?" She usually responds, "Yes, and you've got about five minutes. Wine glasses, the wine, and water need to be brought upstairs."

Upstairs I flip on the television and begin to set up the dining trays. We usually have dinner while watching a variety of shows Debbie enjoys — mostly related to cooking and travel. Once in a while we will check out the Hallmark romances and try to anticipate the recurring plot motifs, almost always the same. CNN is on with Wolf, and I know that is a definite no when we are dining. I hit the button for favorites, and, to my amazement, I see Picasso's "Guernica" dominating the screen. I can't believe it is back in my thinking today. Rick Steves, the travel host is in the Prado in Madrid, and he is giving the viewer a basic explanation of what was behind the creation of the painting. "All set down here," Debbie shouts, and I hold for another moment watching the camera pan slowly over the painting.

"My God," I say to Debbie in the kitchen, "I couldn't believe that Guernica was back in my life today — Rick Steves is in Madrid." My eyes register quickly that tonight is going to be another great dining experience. When we bought this house in Niskayuna in 1986, the only negative that existed for Debbie was the tiny kitchen. I must admit that she got caught up in my enthusiasm about the great back yard framed by pine trees. Over time, the kitchen seemed to become smaller and smaller, yet her culinary skills got better and better, even in the exasperating tight space. Tonight is roast pork with roasted potatoes, roasted onions, roasted broccoli, and roasted butternut squash. As I plate the food, she tells me that the seasoning is garlic, cumin, and garam masala. I take care setting up the food because this is a photograph for FB. "Looks fantastic," I say.

When I get upstairs, I place the food on my tray, pour myself some Assyrtiko, a Greek white, and arrange the tray for a pic. I post the picture on Facebook and label it. I know that there are the regular food connoisseurs who will be on soon to comment. Many of my Facebook friends are familiar with the fact that I often post pictures of meals from home, even take-out with promotions of local restaurants attached.

We end up chatting about an article that Debbie has read in *America* magazine about how Thomas More would view today's world as "Diners, Drive-ins and Dives" rolls past us on the screen. I am savoring the meal, and even though I am not a big fan of meat, these small cuts of pork are cooked just right. Of course, the roast potatoes are the number one ingredient on the plate. I am legendary for the priority of potatoes in a meal. There is something quite amusing between the wonderful meal I am eating and the chicken taco in a converted garage that Guy Fieri is touting on Diners, etc.

The last potato consumed, I pour a little more wine and lean back in the lazy boy chair, feeling so decadent, "God, that was delicious." Debbie smiles and finishes the last bite on her plate. Behind her and asleep on the shawl draped over the back of the chair is Casey. Debbie swings over to Hallmark, and I try to guess whether the predictably handsome guy is the hero or the foil to the hero in tonight's episode, which is at the halfway point. "Hero," Debbie says, confirming my guess. She switches to Mike Calomeco, some type of a food authority, who is midway through his one minute that he has to make some point about food. I feel sorry for him that he is given only one minute — and you can feel the time closing in on him as he rapidly concludes a point about the scarcity of ocean fish, which will necessitate the creation of home-grown fisheries.

"What do you want for dessert?" I say to Debbie affecting seriousness, which is a sort of a recurring joke between us. She pauses, lifts her chin, and says, "Tonight, I think I'll have cake." What makes it funny is that cake is really all we have, except for Stewart's vanilla ice cream. "With ice cream or without?" I ask, and she says, "Without, just a few nuts."

She holds her fork as I gather the plates and head downstairs. Just as I reach the bottom, she says, "Hurry up, Nick is on." Oh, my God, I love Nick Stellino, whose cooking show is entitled "Storyteller in the Kitchen." What makes Nick so appealing is his love of life, from growing up in Sicily with his beloved parents to his love of cooking and sharing his favorite recipes on his show. He often begins each show with the memories of foods he experienced as a child and then speaks of how he evolved in his appreciation and love of food.

In the kitchen, I wash the dishes and prepare the dessert: cake and a few pecans for Debbie; cake and two small scoops of ice cream for me. Returning, I give Debbie her cake — "Looks lovely," she says, — and then I pour each of us another touch of wine and proceed to enjoy dessert. Nick is working on a chicken and pasta dish, loving every moment, and he is about to reach my favorite moment, when he says, "Let me show you to plate." I use the phase all the time when I am in the kitchen pretending, but tonight he says, "Let me show you how to plate this dish." I am disappointed — what seemed natural and so in character now has become the "proper" way to say it.

The phone (landline) rings, its incoming number registering on our television — Avila. It's my brother and I pick up as Debbie lowers the volume on the television. "Just want to see how you're handling all these political shenanigans," he says and we both laugh. "Well," I say, "Trump made another move on the phone to try to talk some sense into the Georgia voting authorities, but that didn't work out too well."

"No, it didn't," Leo says, "not sure what he's got left."

"Well, there's Hawley and Cruz who plan to make a move on Wednesday when the final authorization of the election is made in front of both Houses."

"That will slow things down a bit," Leo says, "but it's really all over."

"Yeah, all is well otherwise?" I ask. Leo lives at Avila, a senior living center, and they have been shut down to outsiders for months — so far, we thank God they have not had any cases of COVID.

"Yup, talked to John (our brother) tonight, and he said as soon as I can to get the vaccine."

"Good idea," I say. "You're almost 90 — they should be coming around soon."

"That's what I say. I have been loosening up my arm — I"m ready."

"Excellent, and I am ready too as soon as I hear it's available."

"Ok," Leo says, "just checking in. Take care of yourself."

"You too, Lee," I say, "talk soon." The pandemic has been tough for all of us, but I think that for people who no longer drive and can't really get out, it has to be really a battle. Leo who loves to gather with people now gets his dinner delivered because the residents can't be together in the dining room.

Debbie has "Cook's Country" on, and one of the two hosts, Bridget Lancaster, is watching one of their young chefs demonstrate how to prepare a veggie lasagna. "Leo ok?" she says.

"Yeah," he's good. "Just chatted about Trump a bit. Hey, I say, switch over to Hallmark, let's see where they are." And voila, the timing is perfect. The romantic lead is heading to the airport so that he can fly to some distant city to accept a major promotion: meanwhile back in the Christmas decorated village, the woman who is meant for him is adjusting to how life will be without him. "You look so sad," her Mom says. At the airport, the lead sees a note that the woman has left him inside his bag. The camera zooms in to a close-up of his face. We know the rest. He returns and meets her while she is out for a walk. I look at Debbie — 7:58 p.m. "He better hurry — he has under two minutes." She laughs as the hero tells the woman that he has thought it over hard, and what is life all about if one isn't happy, and he has never been happier than he is in this town with her. It's 7:59 — she moves in close, and the kiss happens right on time.

Debbie hits the remote and Anderson Cooper is speaking right into the camera about Trump's phone call to Georgia on Saturday. "Well," Debbie says, "I'm heading down."

"Be there in a few," I say, noticing that Casey is sound asleep on the back of her chair. One thing I have noticed is that if I keep the television on, Casey remains asleep, almost as if the TV serves as a narcotic. I have heard the gist of the story that Cooper is doing earlier today, and so I pack up my things — water, dish, and wine glass and head down, leaving the television on. This way, Casey won't bug me for food as soon as I get to the kitchen. In the kitchen, I glance at my cell phone, notice that one of my word friends is waiting for me to make a move. I look quickly, try to see what moves I have, scramble my letters a bit until I see a word, and then play it, while trying to make sure I don't leave any major openings again for a triple word score. I finish the few remaining dishes and head in for the crossword.

Debbie usually retires early — by 9, she is asleep, but she usually is up for a crossword puzzle or two before bed from the *Gazette*. I lean into the bedroom from the doorway. "Up for a puzzle?" She says, "Sure," and I flop onto the bed and prop myself up next to her. She has a backlog of puzzles because some nights she just collapses and falls asleep. We can usually tell right away whether it is a day early in the week or a day late in the week: the later the day of week, the more challenging the puzzle. We are cruising right along when guess who shows up. Casey woke up and realized that he was alone. Usually when he jumps on the bed, his goal is to settle in on top of the blanket covering Debbie. At this hour, I am still considered an intruder. He stares at me as if to say, "You take up an awful lot of room." Reading his mind, I scrunch my body sideways away from them. Debbie is talking to him, and he climbs up and walks toward her face, as she gently slides the puzzle off to her right. "Come on, settle in, Casey. It's all right." And he turns slowly, walks down her body a few paces, and then nestles in with his body kind of between her legs, his butt facing us.

I give him a minute and carefully slide back over as Debbie picks up the puzzle. A couple of answers that hadn't come before now seem apparent when a few of the letters are filled in. We finish and then peek at the day of the puzzle —a Thursday. "Seemed about right," Debbie says. "I think just one puzzle tonight."

Casey has drifted off, and I carefully slide off the bed on my right. He will come later to me for food. Usually about 10:30 and then when I come down for the night, sometime about midnight.

Sitting at my desk, I browse at one of the books I bought today, *A Small Fiction,* a collection of stories of no more than 280 characters. I open the book at random:

"Kiss me," said the frog, "and I'll turn into a prince!"
The princess thought it over.
"I don't see the upside for me here," she said (pg 71).

I chuckle and decide to post a few on Facebook. In a time in which so much contention and depressing material is appearing on FB, I often prefer to post something with a touch of levity or affirmation. After doing that, I jump over to a piece of writing I have been working on. It's about the day I ate a marijuana cookie while visiting a former student and her child. The issue with the story right now is how to capture the total disorientation that I experienced shortly after consuming the cookie, a day when my mind turned to mush and my world became an unfamiliar land. I struggle with the story trying to capture what had happened so that as Hemingway once wrote the reader will have a sense of how I felt at the time. And then I glance at my watch — 11:02 p.m.

I head upstairs to the show that usually concludes my day, "The Eleventh Hour" with Brian Williams. I must admit that I jump around a bit at 11:35 to Colbert and occasionally Fallon and sometimes sports, but I like Williams and his careful preparation, especially with his first three guests. Casey has heard me, arriving quickly at the side of my chair, and is staring up at me, "Please, Sir, can I have some food?" I jump up, "Ok, Casey, quickly." I rush down, and he still beats me to bottom of the stairs.

Some canned food from the fridge and some dry food, and I am back upstairs as Neal Katyal, one of Williams' guests, is responding to some question about a DC judge looking at the idea of insurrection promoted by political leaders. For a second, I check the sports stations and on Channel 25, I find a temptation that can lure me away from most news shows — Ultimate fighting. It appears to be a championship fight — the Flyweight Division — I read the names off the screen: the challenger is Brandon Moreno; the champion is Deiveson Figueiredo. The champion looks bigger and stronger, so my instinct is to go with the challenger. Whoops — Casey has jumped up on my lap, and this will be a bit of a problem because I tend to get into the fights, and he wants to go to sleep.

(It is eleven o'clock at night at our home in Raymertown. About eight years old, I have slipped down the stairs very quietly, the staircase located behind my father's chair. The television is on, and my father, having identified with one of the wrestlers on the screen, is sitting forward in the chair and twisting his body to break free from the hold the other wrestler has on him. I am really looking at three wrestlers, the two on the screen and the double of one, my father, who is trying to recover from the brutal body slams being inflicted on him by someone with a name like Killer Kowalski or Yukon Eric. My father's body recoils as his guy gets a forearm to the throat, but quickly recovers and runs up against the ring ropes, and like an arrow come barreling back to level the opponent. My father is almost on the floor.)

That's why Casey is a problem, because I tend to get into fights too. The fight has started and Deiveson comes right across the ring and begins attacking with vicious kicks and punches. I fear that Moreno, who appears frail in comparison, will not hold up well if this onslaught continues. But he does because he is elusive and even begins an offense of his own, though I breathe with a sigh of relief every time a haymaker just misses Moreno's head. Moreno's survives the first round, and I have some hope.

By the third round, the fight is pretty even. The champion still seems much stronger, but the challenger was able to rush the champion twice and bring him to the canvas. When the challenger started some ground and pound, the champion resorted to some dirty work and poked a finger into the challenger's eye, causing the ref to pause the fight while the challenger recovered. The champion also got a warning. By the fourth round the fight is still very close. I am totally into it, having become my father in my body language. Casey, amazingly, remains sound asleep in my lap.

Round five, and it is very tight. My guy, whose arm seems to be dislocated, takes about five straight lefts to the head — solid shots — but he fights back and almost takes the champion down. At the bell, they are still going full tilt, and I say aloud, "Good Fight!" and Casey looks up at me, and then puts his head back down with a sigh.

Two judges call the fight even, and one judge votes for the champion, resulting in what is called I believe a majority win or something like that. The champion retains his title.

It is midnight, and time to retire. I turn the light to my left off, and then the television with the remote, leaving one light. Casey knows the signals, and hops down to the floor. I hit the final light and descend. It is after midnight when I get his food ready, and he purrs away when I place it in front of him.

I will check Facebook for Tuesday birthdays and wish all a happy birthday. Then I will brush my teeth and climb into bed. I may read one chapter of *On Earth We're Briefly Gorgeous*, and then drift off to sleep.

Tuesday, January 5th, awaits.

Betty Crocker's Recipe

We chuckle sometimes in the car when we sort of forget that we have had our GPS still plugged in, and our road guide says a word that sounds like Shu neck tuddy, and usually we say sometimes simultaneously like stuffy teachers "SCHENECT-ADY!!" as if the lady could hear us correcting her, and then we burst out laughing. But I should act superior? There was a day not too long ago when the word Schenectady appeared as strange to me as the word Scurecgdyatee, even though I had worked in the city my entire professional life. Let me take you back to that day when the world and Schenectady turned into a foreign land.

I hadn't seen Andrea in about a year and a half. I had taught her years ago, and we had kept in touch with Messenger and an occasional coffee or glass of wine when she was in the area. Her life had more than its shares of twists and turns, but she was a fighter and a survivor. Though based in Philadelphia now, she had delivered her baby in a local hospital, and I had popped in on her the day after the birth. Her Mom was there too, and she and I joined with Andrea in her joy over the new baby. She had named him Jude.

After spending a few days of recovering from the birth at her grandmother's, she had returned to Philly where the father had stayed in their apartment. He had some issues, which Andrea wasn't that specific about, but she felt that he would come around eventually and be a good father.

During the year and a half, there were a number of rocky moments which I didn't know that much about, except that her road was tough going. Back in the area again and staying with her grandmother, she had called and said, "Come on out for a visit and see how much Jude has grown." I had been to the house once before to drop off an item that her Grandmother Joyce could give Andrea when she visited her. About a thirty minute drive, I had set out about 12:30 telling Andrea not to worry about lunch, that I would grab something before I got there.

The GPS ran the show for me: Route 90 to 787 heading to Troy, across the Menands Bridge, up the hill to Route 4, past Hudson Valley, left on Williams Road, onto to Whiteview Road, left on Hidley, and then the third house on the left.

As I arrive, Andrea is finishing a cigarette on the front step and lights up with a big smile when I pull in. She flips the smoke into a small can and stands up, "Great to see you, OB. It's been awhile."

We give each other a welcome hug. "Stepped out for a smoke. Gramma doesn't like me smoking and especially smoking in the house. Left Jude in the house —early nap, but I'll wake him for you."

"Please don't," I say. "Let him sleep. I can just look at him."

She laughs and says, "Come on in, and say hello to Gramma."

Joyce is sitting on the sofa with her cat on her lap as we enter. In the crib to her left is the little guy, his face turned toward us, but very much asleep.

"Hi, Paul," Joyce says, "Good to see you." With her words and probably because of a stranger in the room, the cat leaps down and disappears.

"Great to see you," I say. "Looks as if you're the overseer right now for the little guy."

"Oh, the precious little thing — sleeps like a rock, which I love." She looks at Andrea who is standing just off to my right. "As long as this one doesn't feel she has to wake him up."

"But I want Mr. O to see him in action," Andrea says.

Gramma rolls her eyes, "I'll give you action," she says.

We end up having a chat about her backyard gardening, the Mayor of Albany and how she is handling some of the college students in residential homes, and the Yankees and Mets in the pennant race. Jude sleeps through it all. Andrea seems to be getting a little restless and needs more of a one on one talk for a bit.

"Mr. O, how about a coffee and a cookie or two. Sandy was over this morning and dropped off a batch, you know, with her special touch. Gramma, you can go ahead and do your stuff. I can see the crib from the table."

"Good, I do have a few things I need to do," she says as she gets up slowly, while muttering, "Getting old ain't fun."

"Take care," I say to Gramma as she starts to walk past me. I look over at A, "Sounds great to me," I say, "Sandy doing well?"

"She's good. Loves her kid. She does have a lot of shit to deal with at Micky D's — with customers and with management. But she continues to keep her sense of humor. Love her. And she can still whip up her special cookies."

I sit down at the far end of the table with A to my left. She drops a couple of mugs down and says, "I made this coffee about an hour ago, but I think it's still ok."

"Sure, I am not really much of a connoisseur — just cream and fake sugar does it for me."

She laughs and sets down a plate of half a dozen chocolate chips. "Sandy still uses the Betty Crocker recipe," she says and laughs.

"Glad to see that she respects tradition."

She puts down a small plate for each of us and then a glass half filled with milk and a small dish with Sweet and Low. She steps back, grabs the coffee pot, and pours us each a cup. "Leaving you room for milk and sweetener," she says.

"Your choice, Mr. O," as she holds the plate in front of me." I reach for one that is loaded with chips. I take a bite, and the texture is perfect, substantial with an easy give, and I know I catch two or three chips on the first bite. "Very tasty," I say.

Andrea laughs and takes a bite of hers. She chews for a few seconds and then says, "Just to remind you. Sandy has installed her special ingredient in these cookies."

I look at her, still holding the cookie with the one bite out of it. "What's that?"

"What will give the cookie that joyful buzz?"

"She put marijuana in these?" I ask, still holding the cookie in the air.

"Yup, she has her own recipe that blends well with Betty Crocker's."

"Yikes," I say, setting the cookie down on my plate.

Andrea takes another bite, "Ah, so good."

"Well, one cookie can't hurt me that much," I say, picking it up and taking another bite.

I finish the cookie — no way will I try another one, although I am feeling perfectly myself. Fine.

We start chatting about writing and I ask her when she is going to try to tell her story — she's been through so much and managed to stay above water — when my head starts to sway very slowly. I can't get a grip on what's going on, but it kind of feels like my head is encased in an oscillating helmut that is being controlled, independent of my will. I look at Andrea and smile a bit. "You know, I might need a glass of water," I say, thinking that whatever is starting to work on me needs to be diluted.

Andrea places a large glass of water in front of me, and I drink about half of it. "There, that should help," I say.

She smiles and picks up another cookie. I am staring at the crib, and I see that the little guy is twisting around and rolling, sort of a dream-dance but then he seems to settle back down. The room is losing its right angles and becoming more of globe. Andrea's hand is on my left arm, "You ok, OB?" she asks.

"Feel a little fuzzy," I say and pick up the glass of water and finish it. "You know what?" I glance at my watch, "I got a dinner tonight with Leo and Debbie at Avila. I probably should head out."

"Sure," she says, "wanted you to see the little guy awake and active, but next time. Can you make it home all right?"

"I'll just take it easy," I say as I stand and for a moment the room slides to the right.

Gramma has come to the top of the stairs to wave goodbye as Andrea holds the door for me. The sun nearly blinds me as I step out, and I grab the rail along the steps. I get military to reach the car and then in relief flop into the car's darkness. Andrea is standing in the yard as I start the car and open the window, "Great to see you, Andrea, and tell Sandy that I thank her — I think — for the cookie."

She smiles and waves as I back out of the yard by moving the stick to an R.

I am in a machine and moving forward, but I am not sure how. Whoops! A stop sign! Stop!! Geesss! That was a short street! I look both ways. Nothing coming — do I take a right? Not sure. Ok, just go.

I pass a sign that said Whitestone or was it Whiteview? Something about white sounds right. I look at the speedometer. Keep it slow, Buddy. Nothing above 25. Just to be safe. My head feels crinkly — reminds me of a name of a former student — Crinkle — close, but now Crinkly sounds right. Crinkly. I shake it a couple of times.

Wait, how did that White road become Williams Road? That sign — Williams — Ted's — Road. I glance in the rearview mirror — that car is pretty close there behind me — what is that called — tailgating? That's not right. And I'm going — whoops up to 28 — I have to slow down. Off to my right I see a bunch of buildings — look like factories or something. Wait — is that HVCC? I remember because Andrea's grandmother lives out past HVCC. That's it — ok, at this pulsating light, I have to go right.

Is it red — it keeps pulsing beams into my eyes — reds and oranges and yellows — did that turn green or yellow? Maybe. Someone is laying on his horn — "Shut up!" I yell to the tailgater and then I turn right — thank God. How far is home, I wonder

Ah, yes the Valley. Ok, ok, get a grip, Paulie — you're all right. Geeeesss, I'm in the left lane and the arrow is green — down a hill. Oh God, this hill is steep. Keep your foot on the brakes! What's at the bottom? Another light coming — sunglasses! Put them on! They will take care of things. Crap, no better! Still pulsing lights but there's a bridge off to my left. I think I took a bridge to get to Andrea's — it's got to be.

So many cars passing me on the left — what the hell are they all staring at? I'd give them the bird, but I remember the story of this guy who did — and the guy he gave the bird to had a pistol in his front seat — and blasted a hole in the birdman's windshield — didn't kill him, but close. Hold all birds!

Everything seems flat now, spread out. I hold steady at 25 miles an hour — that seems fast enough. The river looks odd down there — awfully brown. A car horn blares! God, pay attention, Paulie. You have one goal — get home. Road sign says 787. Hum 787 — ahhh — could that be right — not sure. Too late — I'm on it now.

I'm on the expressway — can't go above thirty — there's the river again — how did it get so dirty? "Son of a bitch!" Where do these guys passing me think we are — Watkins Glen. Crazy stuff!! What am I doing — 29? That's good — keep it below 30. And keep it together.

Oh my God — more signs. Trog — that sounds familiar. Scureegdyatee blurred— what was that again? Why does that sound familiar? Trog, no Troy — I don't think so — not sure — ah — ok that other place. Phew - a big loop like a ferris wheel onto - what is this? Route 7. Oh my God, they're all speeding again.

My head — crinkly again — it's like when the whole family at Christmas reaches down at the same time and grabs all the wrapping paper from the opened presents and tries to jam the papers into one garbage bag — and that's my head now.

Something tells me to stay on 7 and keep looking for that weird name — Schuree…. Cars flying by and blowing their horns but they no longer bother me — I think — It's like life. You make your choices and find your lane and you're good — screw the rest of these losers!! I'm fine.

The signs are getting harder to read, like the eye doctor's chart once you get past the first two lines — was that a D or an O? An F or an E? Ahhh, sometimes you got to just wing it.

I am not sure how it happened but I made a couple of loops and then came face to face with another light and that S word …. Take a right I say. You're almost home. I keep telling myself that, but I'm not sure where home is exactly. Just stay on the road. And don't SPEED! You don't want to get pulled over — oh, my God!! What if …

"It was just a small marijuana cookie, officer. And I was very careful driving — you know, officer, there are a lot of big-time speeders out there today."

Mercedes Benz Dealership — yes — that rings a bell. You're going to make it, Paulie. Wait! — there's the place with the bowling alley bar — Innovo. Rosetti — I know that guy. You had lunch last week there with him. Rich, the guy you taught.

The Mobile Gas Station! — yes — so close, get over, Paulie. I can't — too late —someone's out there. Stop beeping! I am going to have to take my next right and turn around. These speeders — Christmas — ok, that's it. All set now. Look both ways. Nothing. Go. Go!!

The garage door opens — how did that happen? I enter the darkness of home. Inside, CT looks at me and says, "I could use a treat." I look back. "CT, you will have to wait. I got to sack it. I have to get sober for tonight's dinner."

The whole room is spinning as my head hits the pillow. "Oh my God," I say, "I better set the alarm for tonight's dinner or I may never wake up." But I can't figure out how to set the alarm, and as my head falls back on the pillow, the room tips over, and I'm gone.

Lives from Notre Dame and Notre Dame-Bishop Gibbons

I loved my years teaching at Notre Dame and Notre Dame-Bishop Gibbons, and I always enjoy getting together with grads to talk about their journeys and then tell them about the present state of the school. When I joined Facebook, my link to graduates increased dramatically, and I was able to stay in touch with many through messaging and posting their successes and the school's successes, whether it be scholarships won, mock trial victories, National Honor Society Dinners, sports' victories, theater productions. I also enjoy posting pictures from old yearbooks, which grads really seem to appreciate. In writing this new book about the next stage of life, I thought that it would be good to choose a few grads and see if I could tell their story, their journey, and their memories. The eight I reached were all willing and eager to share their journey. The process involved a few steps: I prepared a sheet of questions that they could look over, questions about their memories of high school, their choice of career, significant relationships, key transitional moments along the way, and personal interests like the place of music, travel, pets, etc in their lives. Then we agreed upon a date for a phone call, which I would tape. Our conversations usually ran about an hour, and I took notes in addition to the taping. From my material, I sent follow-up questions — further clarification or topics that needed amplification for example — and when I got those responses, I wrote a draft. Once done, I emailed the draft to the person, and he or she made any corrections or additions they wished. Then I did a final draft weaving in the changes and sent that draft back for approval. Overall, I am pleased with the results. I have two grads from the 70's, three from the 80's, one from the 90's, and two from the current century, roughly spanning 50 years. There are four women and four men.

MARYANNE PANARESE VERMILLION

Underneath MaryAnne's senior picture in the 1975 *Prelude*, we see the words of Oliver Wendell Holmes, Sr., "A moment's insight is sometimes worth a life's experience." Unlike many quotations under graduate pictures in high school yearbooks, MaryAnne's choice seems both apropos and prescient. From Bridgeport, Connecticut, to Phoenix, Arizona, MaryAnne's journey has been marked by moments that transformed her vision and illuminated the road she traveled.

One moment took place in English class at Notre Dame as she sat with other students in English reading *Our Town* by Thornton Wilder. She recalled that the teacher had forgotten his book that day and was kneeling on the floor gazing over her shoulder at her book. It was Act III, and Emily, who has been granted a chance to return to life for one day, is speaking to the Stage Manager. MaryAnne remembers clearly Emily's line, "Do any human beings ever realize life while they live it? —- every, every minute?" She remembers the teacher reaching over her shoulder and pointing at that line and saying, "Key." That line from the play never left MaryAnne's mind. She has another moment from high school etched indelibly in her mind and soul. In religion class the students had been asked to look up "The Resurrection of Lazarus." As she read the account of Lazarus, she stopped at one line — "Jesus wept." And with those two words her whole view of religion shifted. That line opened up her faith to the humanity of Jesus. And it was that faith strengthened by her grasp of who Jesus was — how human He was — that helped to carry her through many of the struggles of life to come.

"My high school years at Notre Dame were wonderful," MaryAnne recounts. Not all students loved the modular approach to learning, which allowed for a variety of learning models: traditional class, small group, individualized instruction, but for MaryAnne it was ideal. "I liked the choice, and I liked independent study projects. One I recall was my creation of a major journal on Mark Twain under the guidance of Sister Mary Lucey. I learned so much about Twain." She remembers Father Robert Nugent with his silver, gold, and blue cleric shirts, clothing that did not please MaryAnne's Mom — "Priests wear black!" her Mom would say. He was her theology teacher for two years. "He was very spiritual. There was always an invitation for us students to come to the Lord's table and share in the Mass with him. He made the Mass a special and personal experience." MaryAnne will also never forget Father Nugent's intensity about one exclamation they should never utter — "God Damn!" To him, it was the most egregious example of using the Lord's name in vain. "He asked us to think about what we were saying. We were asking God to damn someone or something. Who were we? God? Calling on God and telling him what to do. I will never forget this moment. From that time on, I didn't allow or tolerate that exclamation being said in my presence, and I've stood up to my former in-laws for saying it."

Prior to attending Notre Dame, MaryAnne spent her early years in Bridgeport, Connecticut, before her parents moved to Ballston Lake in 1968, and she began to attend St. Helen's School. She was fourteen when her parents divorced, and she had the one parent for the rest of her formative years. MaryAnne's Mom, Vera, was a strong person and, in some ways unbending, but, for the most part, she set an example for MaryAnne. "She taught me how I'd have to live in a world much bigger than me. I was not to be afraid to speak up, volunteer or do something that I wanted. Sometimes she stopped me, but ninety percent of the time she pushed me to 'go for it.' She sacrificed a lot in her life for me, especially after my father left. We stayed in New York where I was in school and later teaching instead of going back to Connecticut, which everyone knew she wanted to do. She never really tried to rebuild a life for herself, even when she was asked out because she didn't want to disrupt my life."

After high school, the world of education played a major role in the next two decades of MaryAnne's life. She attended Maria College and then completed a degree in elementary education at Cortland. Upon graduating, she took a position at St. Patrick's Grade School in Troy where she spent 15 years teaching. MaryAnne recalls that the students at St. Pat's had a lot of issues, but she had an advantage. "Because I am a little person, the students couldn't always tell whether I was an adult or a kid, and consequently they shared a lot with me." One of MaryAnne's favorite expressions which she gleaned from one of the nuns at St. Pat's was, "Jesus, Mary, and Good Saint Anne," an expression she still uses today. She has strong memories of those years, "I loved the kids and to this day miss that world of teaching."

Life is not always a smooth path, and MaryAnne had some serious health issues. In 1982 she was flown from St. Clare's Hospital to Johns Hopkins for back surgery. "I had lost the use of my right leg, one of the effects of spinal stenosis." It was a time when she relied a great deal on her Faith and her trust in God to see her through the ordeal. After all, she had so much yet to do in her life.

In 1984 she began to organize what would eventually become the Mohawk Valley Chapter of Little People of America. She ran monthly meetings of those she had recruited, organized the sending out of newsletters, and ran fund-raisers — all for the purpose of getting out the word and building membership. During this period, John McLoughlin of Channel 10 was a great help in publicity, even interviewing MaryAnne on television to help promote the cause. Once all the ground work was done, the organization applied for a charter, and in July, 1986, at the National Convention in Dearborn, Michigan, the Charter was granted.

In July of 1989 MaryAnne had one of those fortuitous moments that gave her hope. Father Tony Diacetis had been installed as the new pastor of Our Lady of Grace in Ballston Lake, which was MaryAnne's parish. It was a time when she had been struggling with work issues, issues that might jeopardize her future at St. Pat's. On a day off from her job at the day care center, she went to Mass only to find out that there wasn't a Mass that day. Father Tony was in the Church and MaryAnne introduced herself. "We were having some small talk when he said, 'You look upset about something. Are you ok?' I burst into tears, and he led me into his office, where we had a good talk." What struck her most about Father Tony that day was that "he listened." He helped her to navigate some of the work issues she was dealing with and that September she returned to St. Pat's.

That day was the beginning of their friendship. The relationship grew. Father Tony would often come to the house to visit MaryAnne and her Mom. In many ways, MaryAnne says, "He was like an older brother that I never had." And in October of 1991 Father Tony officiated at MaryAnne's wedding to Larry Yakubowski at Our Lady of Grace Church in Ballston Lake. Larry lived in Phoenix and worked in shipping and receiving for the Cendant Corporation which owned a number of hotels, and so MaryAnne moved to Phoenix to begin the next stage of her life.

Larry and MaryAnne were together for 15 years, but things don't always work out, and as MaryAnne put it, we "unfortunately divorced," though they have remained friends. After a period of time, she met Mark Vermillion, a chemical engineer retiree. In April of 2015 they were married in Phoenix. MaryAnne pointed out that Mark is 6 feet one, and in the world of little people, their marriage would be considered a mixed marriage. For MaryAnne, the marriage has been a wonderful blessing. Not only did she find a soulmate, but she also now has a family of stepchildren, grandchildren, and even great grandchildren, Corbin and Chloe. She loves having a family and being called "Grammy."

During her years in Phoenix, MaryAnne was actively building community. As a member of the Phoenix Chapter of Little People in America, MaryAnne led a mentoring program, similar to a big brothers/ big sisters program, that paired off an adult with an LP (little person) child for questions and guidance. At the annual picnic, she was approached by a gentleman from Tucson who inquired about how one could start the ball rolling on establishing a chapter in his city. Once MaryAnne knew there was a real interest in Tucson, she went to work. "It took organizing and paperwork and pretty much most of the work was done online and through email." In the summer of 2008, "We got the Tucson Charter at the National Convention in Detroit."

Though MaryAnne has struggled with a number of surgeries as well as breast cancer — a proud survivor — she has remained very active at the Church she and Mark attend, St. John the Baptist. She has served as lector, Eucharistic minister, member of the liturgical planning team, money counter, funeral brunch cook and baker ... you name it, MaryAnne is available. She is also a member of the prison ministry team that reaches out to the Perryville Women's Prison in Goodyear, Arizona. One of the things her team does is recognize each prisoner's birthday by sending a card with a scripture verse and a short greeting. She also has a few inmates she communicates with as pen pals. MaryAnne points out that "These women are so grateful to receive a card or kind word. Each month we get numerous thank you notes saying no one remembered me but you."

In 2019, the ministry extended their reach to the children of incarcerated parents, which allowed the children to attend Camp Genesis in Prescott, AZ, for one week in June. The ministry team provides each child upon arrival a backpack filled with toiletries, beach towels, a children's Bible, and journal. The team follows up by sending cards to each child during the year on special occasions such as Halloween and Christmas. MaryAnne finds a special joy in making homemade cards for those children on her list.

MaryAnne has always done so much for others, and I asked her what are some of the ways she celebrates herself. She laughed and said, "Well, I have an eight-year-old rescued Chihuahua named Teddy and a four-year-old rescued Chihuahua/Dachshund mix named Daisy." Of the fun things that she and Mark do together, nothing ranks higher than seeing Elvis impersonator Chance Tinder. MaryAnne had first seen Chance — pre-Mark — at a night out for the Phoenix Little People Chapter. "That night I got scarfed like at a real Elvis concert," and over the years she has accumulated a "collection of scarves and even a Teddy Bear that Chance threw out at the audience while singing the song." Of course, MaryAnne was eager to share Chance with Mark, and now Chance's concerts are their number one favorite date night. "For me Chance sings "Burning Love" better than Elvis did, and for Mark it's "Can't Help Falling in Love With You."

MaryAnne's life has been marked by challenges, and each time she has responded with determination and courage. She has had her share of dark moments but has found strength in her God and in those who cared. She has come to see that one needs to live life to its fullest. And that means including those with whom you share the journey. "Always think of others and what you can do for them even if it's a simple hello." It's back to those moments that matter. In a way she may be an exception to Emily's sense in *Our Town* that humans don't appreciate what they have. MaryAnne has worked hard at seeing and appreciating others each day because she knows that so many are thirsting for that one moment of recognition.

⟶≫ ♦ ≪⟵

JACK RIGHTMYER

"How blessed I am." No four words could better express how Jack Rightmyer feels about his life at this point in time. Husband, father, grandfather, teacher, writer, and runner: Jack has led a full and rich life. "Sure I have minor regrets," Jack says, but "what really matters and what I have come to realize is how much I love family — my mom and dad, my sister, Judy, my two kids, my grandchild." This love of family grounds Jack in his vision of life.

Jack's professional life has been dedicated to teaching and writing. "I could never really decide whether I was more of a teacher or a writer," he says. Jack's teaching career in high school and middle school spanned thirty-nine years, and he has continued that career after retiring from Bethlehem Middle/High School by taking a position as an adjunct in the English Department at Siena College, where he also mentors student teachers. Writing has also been a major part of his life. The author of two books, Jack has a novel he hopes to publish soon and another novel in the works. Jack has been a free-lance journalist for most of his life and for the last few years has been a book reviewer for the Albany *Times Union* and a writer of features and profiles for *Adirondack Sports and Fitness*. Prior to that Jack wrote frequently for the *Daily Gazette* and for a period of time worked as a writer for the Diocesan newspaper, *The Evangelist*. He is rarely without a writing project of some sort or another.

In the challenging days of the pandemic, Jack was still able to forge ahead with his reviewing and his feature writing. His teaching and his work with student teachers at Siena shifted to virtual teaching. Although Jack misses the presence of students, he has adjusted quite well to the technology now employed for teaching. "I have also been very fortunate being married to Judy (a nurse) because she makes sure that we follow the COVID guidelines very closely, and with all the proper precautions I do see my daughter and granddaughter often. I regret, however, that I haven't seen my son Paul (a teacher in Colorado) since Christmas of 2019." Jack says that over the past year he felt an angst about our country and the way it was responding to COVID. He recalls hearing stories about his grandparents during World War II when there was a shortage of goods and the necessity of gas rationing, but the stories revealed how people worked together for the good of all and got the job done. "I was really concerned about the way some people were responding during the pandemic, but now with the vaccine and the new administration, I have more hope."

Jack has always been a glass half full guy and also a person blessed with a marvelous sense of humor, an ability to look at almost any situation and say something clever and witty, never mean-spirited, that brings a smile to the faces of people he is with and often a great laugh. That comic vision was nurtured by a close group of friends Jack had at Notre Dame-Bishop Gibbons, friendships that have lasted. "When I turned 60, seven of us got together at Loon Lake and we had a great time." Jack laughs when he recalls first getting to know in freshman homeroom the student who would eventually become his brother-in-law, Jim Litynski . "If I was four foot eleven and ninety five pounds, Jim was five foot even and ninety eight pounds." One moment in particular stands out in Jack's memory. "Jim walked in one morning early in the fall wearing a George McGovern button, and everybody started making fun of him. I was too afraid to say anything at the time, but after class, I walked up to him and quietly said, 'Hi, I'm Jack,and I like McGovern too.'"

Laughter was the magnet that drew Joe, Mike, Mark, Jim, Beau, Chris and Jack together. "We thought we were so cool talking about things like old 'Twilight Zone' episodes or Carl Sagan, but we were really a bunch of geeks." What was for them a gift from the gods was the modular scheduling that had been established with the merger of Notre Dame and Bishop Gibbons. Jack laughs and says, "For us this was hangout time, and we loved it. We were never mean or sarcastic to each other, more like goofy." One day, however, Jack took some razzing when he wore a pair of shoes his Mom had bought him — penny loafers. "They were unrelenting in teasing me. I remember when I got home, I said to my Mom, 'I can't go back to school wearing these.'"

Jack recalls vividly his first day of high school which started out as a disaster but turned into the beginning of a relationship that helped to shape his future. Realizing in first period that he did not have his locker key, Jack went to the main office to report his missing key. The secretary directed him to Vice

Principal Brother Mostyn, who after hearing of the problem, smiled, put out his hand and said, "Well, Jack, congratulations. You've set the all-time record for losing a locker key." Jack felt some relief, and as they walked together with the new key back to Jack's locker, Brother mentioned that if Jack's desire to be a basketball star didn't work out that he would be welcome to join the track team. A couple of months later after Jack was cut from the hoop team, he signed up for indoor track. Brother Mostyn never failed to encourage Jack in each race he ran, and in senior year Jack broke the school record for the two-mile run. Six years later, Jack coached the Notre Dame-Bishop Gibbons Cross Country Team to the Section Two Class A Cross Country Championship. Jack would continue on to coach cross country during his entire teaching career, with most of his career as the Coach of the Girls' Cross Country team at Bethlehem High School. It all started with the loss of a locker key.

"When I entered high school," Jack says, "I was a blank slate. I mean I liked sports, I liked to write, and come up with stories." Then I had Brother Ray Smith for English, and his classes were so exciting and creative. He actually seemed to love what he was doing, and he loved the literature he was teaching. He was aware of the latest books, he played music in class — Dylan, Young, Simon and Garfunkel, and he even brought films into class, like *2001 A Space Odyssey*." Jack's father, a business man, had started talking to Jack about a career and told him that because Jack was pretty good with numbers maybe a business career would be right up his alley. "But I was watching Brother Smith and he was having a blast teaching literature." When Jack left high school, the slate was no longer blank — "I loved literature and I loved running." In those two loves was Jack's future: at Notre Dame-Bishop Gibbons, Pinkerton Academy in New Hampshire, Bethlehem Middle and High School, and now at Siena College.

To teach well takes time, and it takes trial and error. In his book *A Funny Thing About Teaching*, Jack wrote about his first year as a teacher. The difficulty he found grew out of his own insecurity as a twenty-two year old teaching students who were only a few years younger than he. Another issue was his knowledge of the subject matter. "Although I had received decent grades in college, I suddenly saw that there was an awful lot I didn't know." He struggled to find his way, and what he thought was his lowest point came when he was observed for the first time in early November by Paul O'Brien, the chair of the department. Jack was teaching *Huckleberry Finn*, which was not going well, so he decided to try to break the students up into groups and have them "answer questions about how they faced prejudice." The groups were not cooperative and whined about not being grouped with their friends. Jack kept running around trying to put out fires. When the bell rang, he assumed that his career was over. Paul suggested they meet the next day to discuss the class. Jack nodded but thought that he "would begin looking that night for a job at McDonald's or Pizza Hut." To his astonishment, the meeting with Paul the next day gave him hope. After agreeing that the kids were a bit unruly, Paul pointed out some of the positives he saw including Jack's willingness to take a risk in having kids talk about prejudice they had experienced. Paul also invited Jack to sit in on a few of his classes. Jack did follow up and one thing he noticed in Paul's class was that laughter, Jack's natural gift, could play an essential role in teaching. Jack kept working hard at his job, and a couple weeks before Christmas even smiled a few times while teaching his classes.

A successful teacher of English should be a strong reader. Among his favorite authors are Ray Bradbury, Steven King, and Raymond Carver. "I have a picture of Ray Bradbury in my writing room at home. I started reading him maybe in seventh or eighth grade — *The Martian Chronicles* —and was drawn to his descriptive style and his ability to open up worlds I hadn't thought of before. Of course *Fahrenheit 451* — what a scary world there." Jack recognized early that Steven King was more than just a good story teller. "He was a heck of a good writer, and I read a lot of his books. His book *11/22/63* did such a great job of capturing the world at the time of the assassination of JFK." And Raymond Carver is one of Jack's favorites: "I know those people in his stories. In my Dad's family. At weddings I attended. Carver has caught them."

Certainly the phrase *carpe diem* fits Jack's approach to life. "We don't know how long we have. We can't settle for just getting by, we have to go for it." This thought is reinforced by one of Jack's favorite quotations from *The Shawshank Redemption* when Andy says to Red, "Get busy living or get busy dying." Jack is also a firm believer in the idea of using the gifts you were given. He loves the quotation from Eric Liddell in *Chariots of Fire* who misses a prayer meeting and runs instead. Liddell feels that not to honor his gift would be to dishonor God, "I believe that God made me for a purpose. But he also made me fast, and when I run, I feel His pleasure."

Another way to think about *carpe diem* is to think about what gives one pleasure in the quiet moments that are so vital in life. For Jack, it is walking the neighborhood with their dog Abe, a faithful and gentle giant who will sit quietly and wait if Jack meets a neighbor and chats a bit. A perfect retreat for Jack and Judy is to head up to Loon Lake where Judy's family has a house. Snowshoeing, cross country skiing, hiking with Abe during the day, and then a fire and a good book at night. Life at its best.

Jack likes to begin his literature course at Siena with Raymond Carver's story "Cathedral." In the story, the narrator, somewhat narrow-minded, comes to understand Robert, a blind man, a bit more when he shares with Robert near the end of the story with his own eyes closed the action of drawing a cathedral together. In that action, the narrator begins to see. "I love this story," Jack says, "because it gets at the idea of connecting. The older I get the more I see that it is all about connecting with others." Jack remains haunted by a colleague he had worked with who was suffering loneliness and severe depression. He committed suicide, but there was such an outpouring of people at his funeral service. "I wish he had known how much he was loved. I have been so fortunate," Jack says,"I have received so much love from the students I have taught, and the runners I have coached."

Jack has dreams and hopes, one that he get his novel published, but he knows that his life has been a good one and that he will continue to appreciate each moment he is given. 'Yes," he says, "I have been blessed."

———————

I must share a story — two tiered —about Jack that brings a smile to my face whenever I think of it.

Part I: It was sometime in the spring of 1983 — perhaps a Wednesday. The Albany Diocese was having their annual Conference for Catholic School Teachers, and it was being held in the Conference Center at the Empire State Plaza. Most of the teachers carpooled. Jack told me that he would be happy to drive. Two other teachers asked to join us. Jack would pick up me and one of the two — Tony — at ND-BG, and then the other teacher in Albany. When we got into the car at school, I in the front and Tony in the back, Tony, a dignified and mild-mannered chemistry teacher, said, "Jack,

I see that your warning light for oil is on. You should probably check that." Jack responded and said, "Yeah, I'll check that a little later." Then we settled in for the trip. When we got to Dom's apartment in Albany, he asked us to come in for coffee. After coffee, Dom brought out a bottle of vintage red wine and some cheese and crackers. "We can slip in a little late," he said. About noon, I think it was Jack who said, "Anyone up for lunch?" We all laughed, and Dom said, "There's a good spot over on Delaware Avenue. When we got into the car, Tony noticed that the warning light had come on again. "Jack," his voice had more authority in it now, "you better check your dam oil level." Jack laughed and said, "Ahh, she'll be fine." During our hearty lunch accompanied by more wine, we agreed that it was much too late for the Conference and settled in to enjoy the rest of the meal. Reaching the car for the trip home, Jack had no sooner turned the car on than Tony saw the light and burst out, "JACK, WILL YOU CHECK THE F____ing OIL!" We didn't stop laughing for the rest of the trip!

Part II: It was a few months later, and Jack was on the way home to Latham, but he had to make a stop at the Colonie Mall. When he pulled into the Mall, he saw a lot of people waving at him because, he guessed, maybe he had a cool looking car, so he waved back at them, even gave a thumb's up, not knowing he had flames pouring out the bottom of his car. Someone called the fire company, and the trucks arrived to put out the flames. Jack knew he was going to be late, so he called his Mom to tell her he had been delayed. She said, "Thanks for calling, Jack, but whatever you do, stay away from the Colonie Mall. News reports say there is a car on fire there."

LARRY BARRY

You might say that in some ways Larry Barry is locked in. His day begins with his 8 a.m. alarm. Out of bed, he does a sit-up routine to get loosened up. By 9 a.m. he is on the treadmill at his brother Kevin's house, a machine they both share. After an hour, sometimes an hour and a half, of fast walking often at an incline, Larry heads home for a light breakfast of oatmeal and perhaps a banana. After a shower, he leaves home at 11:15, arriving at the Federal Court House in Albany where he works as security guard beginning at 11:45. After checking in, he relieves the other guard and assumes his detail in the guard house for the next two hours. He keeps his eyes on the flow of pedestrian traffic, which includes staff, judges, defendants, attorneys, and other civilians coming to the courthouse. After two hours, he switches position with another guard and moves outside to the front of the courthouse where he spends an hour of patrol and then moves back to the guard house, switching each hour until his day ends when he signs out at 5:54 p.m. He is home by 6:20 and proceeds to share in the preparation of dinner with his Mom. She usually gets the salad and the veggies ready, and he works the grill. One or two nights a week, Larry drives to his girlfriend Jackie's house and has dinner with her and watches a little television. For the weekends, he drives home, drops off his gun, gathers his clothes, and heads to Jackie's.

Jackie is a major reason Larry feels good about his life right now. Although he had known her for many years as a neighbor in his Rotterdam community, he had not seen her in nearly ten years until she showed up at the wake for his father. He recalled saying when she approached him in line, "Well, here's a blast from the past." A few days after the funeral, Larry called Jackie to see if she might want to go out for a drink and a bite to eat. Two things happened that night to endear Larry to Jackie. At Bombers in downtown Schenectady, she asked him if he preferred the bar or a booth. He said a booth would be fine, and she was pleased because the last couple of guys she had dated had wanted to sit at the bar and then tended to drink too much. As they were about to cross the street after, Larry took her hand, and Jackie felt right at that moment that she was with a special guy. They have now been dating for over three and a half years. A long-time medical assistant to a rheumatologist and also a phlebotomist, Jackie is the mother of a sixteen-year-old girl. Once Amber has finished high school and gets herself situated, Larry and Jackie would like to move to Florida and bask in the warmth of the sun.

Larry had experienced a year in Florida shortly after he retired from the New York State Department of Corrections in 2015, after 26 years of service. He loved Florida, but had to return home to help out with his Dad who was being placed in a nursing home. Larry recalls his Dad's early influence in the way Larry thought about his choice of career. "My father told us to find a job that had a good pension." I looked at a number of the Civil Service exams and took for a starter the one for the Post Office. My grade wasn't quite to their standard, and so I took a review course to improve the grade. In the meantime, I had taken the one for Corrections and been accepted. Four weeks into the Academy training for Correction officers, I got mail indicating that I had a score in the mid-90's in the Postal test. I debated it, and then decided to stick with Corrections because I was four weeks in and liked the guys I was in school with." Over his 26 years in Corrections, Larry spent time working in a number of prisons starting in Green Haven and ending — in his longest time working at a prison — 15 years — at Five Points Correctional Facility.

Larry made a number of lasting friends among guards he worked with, some of whom were on multiple Myrtle Beach golfing trips, like Bill Cullen, Bruce Shafer, and David Mosher, but his strongest memories of the world of corrections have to do with sudden loss and in one case the justice system when it did not seem to work at its best. On one particular day as he was leaving work, Larry said goodbye to Mark M., one of the officers who worked the perimeter of the prison. Shortly after Larry left, Mark got in the facility perimeter vehicle and pulled out of the prison right into the path of a tractor trailer. The big truck T-Boned him, but it didn't kill him. The superintendent of the prison was a few cars behind the big rig and saw it happen, but the next part was even worse. A woman coming the other way stopped and got out of her car to try to help. As she approached, Mark who was lying on the ground seriously injured pulled out his duty weapon and killed himself. An investigation revealed that he had been having an affair and was wracked with guilt. "To see him one moment and wave good-bye and then a short time after to know that he had killed himself was tough." Rich Norton, another guard, was a good friend for 18 years or so, and he had accompanied Larry and his golfing buddies a number of times to Myrtle Beach, always a lot of fun. Rich was in the hospital for a minor operation, and "I had called to see how he was doing. He seemed fine, and asked me if I could stop in the office at work and pick up his paycheck." Larry did and when he got to the hospital, he asked for Rich, and the nurse said, "Are you family?" Larry said no, and asked why. "Rich has died, getting out of bed, a blood clot." Larry said that he walked out to his car and just sat there, one of his best friends, gone in an instant.

Aaron East was an inmate who worked for Larry when Larry ran the Infirmary at Five Points. "He was an excellent worker, was on a task almost before I assigned it, earning his 20 cents an hour." Aaron's story was a tough one too. He had been part of a group that was involved in a hate crime that involved stomping a man to death. Because Aaron had not actually done any of the stomping, though he was by no means innocent, his lawyer told him not to take a plea bargain — "you didn't do it." Aaron was found guilty, and the sentence was 25 to life. The irony is that the one who had actually led in the stomping did plea bargain and got out in ten years. When Larry retired, Aaron had put in twenty two of the twenty five years. Larry still wonders whatever happened to Aaron. Did he ever make it out?

Looking back on the early days of his journey, Larry becomes animated as he recalls the place that sports, friends, family, and school played in his life. His love of sports is linked to his memories of friends from high school. My high school friends were Brian Rucinski, Tim Brady, Preston

Young, Mike Jackson, and Shawn Baker." Bowling was a sport he had done with his family and so it was an easy transition. "I bowled for four years at Gibbons. The bowling alley was right down the street. In those days, bowling was pretty big, and I remember riding in the van sitting with Mike heading to Sectionals — that was so cool." Larry found Preston's humor and easy going qualities very appealing. "He didn't take life too seriously. It's awesome that after 42 years we are still great friends. We both drive Corvettes and we love to show them off." Baseball offered more intensity and at times tested Larry's mettle. "Shawn was an excellent player, the best on the team, and Brian was a heck of a pitcher." The game that Larry can't forget was a double-header against Power Memorial Academy. "I was catching and that day I forgot my cup. I took a couple of low ones, and then at one point in the first game I was run over at home plate." In the break between the games, one of the players asked Larry if he could go in the second game, and Coach said, "Sure, he's fine. Larry, just rub some dirt on it."

Like many students, Larry recalled with fear and admiration math teacher Tom Maguire. "Even though he was short, you knew you didn't mess with him. And he didn't miss a trick. One year in summer school, I had to take a math class. I remember that he would stick with you on a problem until you understood." The course that Larry recalls as having the most impact on him was a semester course in history taught by Ron Cichinelli. "The whole course was on the Kennedy assassination, and did I ever get hooked on that. Growing up, the two historical events in my house were Pearl Harbor and the Kennedy Assassination, and now I had a whole course on it. We watched and analyzed in detail the Zapruder film and studied all the minute details about the location of the shooting. The Book Depository is on my bucket list to visit some day. When Stephen King wrote *11/22/63*, I bought the book the day it came out."

Mentioning Stephen King triggers another thought in Larry's mind, this time including his beloved Boston Red Sox. "My uncle had gotten four tickets to a game at Fenway. I remember that night too because I had gotten black and white film for my camera, just to try something different. Well, about ten seats over from us holding a glove in one hand and a book in the other sat Stephen King. I noticed that at the end of each team's at bat, he would take out his score card and mark it. It was so cool to see him there." Larry had become a Red Sox fan at the age of ten — he recalls the 75 World Series. "I think part of the reason was to be contrary — I wanted to be the opposite of my father who was a Yankee fan, and also across the street were the Deubels who were big Red Sox fans. Chris Deubel and I were good buddies, and we did the whole baseball card thing too — trading for the best players." When Larry thinks about the Red Sox, he has his all-time low moment and his all-time exquisite high moment. "The all-time low moment was Game 7 of the ALCS when Aaron Boone hit the walk-off home run against Tim Wakefield in the 11th inning. That was so tough, but how sweet 2004 was. We were down 3 games to 0, and in the ninth, we were trailing and they had the unbeatable Mariano Rivera on the mound. We all thought it was over, and then somehow we managed to score a run to tie it in the ninth. And then in the twelfth, David Ortiz hits a two-run walk-off home run. And then we win four straight — first time in the history of the playoffs that a team down 0-3 comes back to win the series."

Asked who his all-time favorite Red Sox player is, Larry answered without hesitation, "Dwight Evans — good hitter with a gun for an arm." But one special quality stands out for Larry about Evans. "We were at a Red Sox game, and after the game Dad pointed down at the field and said, 'That guy Evans is pretty special — he is the only one left signing autographs.' And he stayed there until the last fan was gone. Dad was right." And if you have any doubts about Larry's loyalty to the Red Sox, check out the Red Sox logo tattooed on his right arm.

The Celtics and the Bruins are two other Boston teams high on Larry's list: the Celtics with their great teams of Bird, McHale, and Parrish and the epic battles with LA and Magic and Kareem; the Bruins and the night he and Kevin drove to the old Boston Garden to see his team play Game 5 of the Stanley Cup Finals. Shifting cities, another team that ranks way up there for Larry is the Washington Redskins, a long time favorite of his Dad's. Though the team is no longer using the team name "Redskins," that's what Larry will remember them by with his plethora of jerseys and memorabilia from some of his favorite teams. "We were lucky to see them win three Super Bowls — 1983, 1988, and 1992. What was amazing is that it was done with three different starting quarterbacks, and Joe Gibbs was the Coach for each Super Bowl team."

For college hoop, Siena stands alone in the Barry family. "My Dad got us interested in Siena basketball. We would follow Dad in the parking lot to the gym — it seemed a mile away — and he in his Russian hat would be power walking as we ran behind him. Maybe the most exciting year was the 1993-94 season when Siena went 25-8 and made the NIT Tournament. After home game wins over Georgia Tech and Tulane, "We made the trip to Madison Square Garden where we lost to a very good Villanova team. I get chills thinking of that experience."

Music has always been huge for Larry from his first concert of Ozzie Osborne with his friend Mike Jackson to MTV bursting on the scene with such great songs as David Lee Roth's "California Girls," to some of his favorite heavy metal bands — Motley Crew, Rat Poison, Slayer — to one of the best concerts he ever saw — Billy Joel and Elton John in front of 80 thousand fans at Giants Stadium. And when you combine music with some of Larry's cars — the 68 Plymouth Valiant, the 67 Catalina — the boat, and then his first great sports car — a Trans Am, you put the man in heaven. Go one notch higher and you have Larry fulfilling his dream of owning a Corvette. After years of research and scouring hundreds of ads, "I pulled the trigger on Memorial Day weekend of 2019, and Jackie and I drove to Rhode Island to pick it up" — a torch red 2012 Chevy Corvette Grand Sport, with a 6.2 liter engine and 455 horses. "It is dream to drive." And when Larry wants to unwind in his car after a hard day's work, he has two songs that get him to where he needs to be: "Wash It All Away" by Five Finger Death Punch and "I'm Shipping Up to Boston" by Dropkick Murphy.

No question, Larry would say that life is good. Coming up is a trip on December 26th to Disney World — a Christmas present to Amber from Jackie and Larry, and then in September a trip to Hawaii with Jackie, a place that Larry has been to twice before and loves. He definitely has a few keys left on his bucket list, but he is proud of having achieved one major item on the list — he and Kevin taking their Dad to South Bend to see the Notre Dame Fighting Irish.

That dream got solid footing when a doctor Kevin worked for offered him tickets for Notre Dame's opening game of the 2011 season. The journey remains sharp and clear in Larry's mind. Stopping about an hour short of South Bend, they registered at a hotel and then set out for dinner, and in a little one-horse town about 30 minutes away, they found a magical restaurant with its menu written out in chalk on the wall. The meal — delicious steaks with complimentary apple pie. "As Kevin drove away, I looked back and the town disappeared into the corn fields. Were we ever really there?" The magic continued as they arrived in South Bend on a very warm 80 plus day. As Kevin was getting their father settled in, "I had a chance to go inside the golden dome and see its ceiling painted in magnificent colors." Back at the Stadium, they had seats up high, and in the heat rapidly consumed the bottles of water they had purchased. The game itself had an unfortunate twist when Florida recovered a fumble on their own one yard line and ran the ball back 99 yards for a touchdown. Just before half with dark clouds rolling in, their father headed down to find some coolness. The rain started and Larry said,"It felt good. Kevin and I were excited because the ND Marching Band was about to perform." However, fate was not with the Barrys that day — the clouds grew more menacing and the Band and the fans were asked to evacuate and find shelter. Having gathered in the Joyce Center with their Dad, they noticed that the weather forecast was looking grimmer and so decided to head back to the hotel. There, they discovered that the game had restarted and then the stands evacuated again. The game was finally restarted and after seven hours, it ended with ND losing. "As I look back, the score didn't matter. We were able to get Dad to see a home game and even though they lost we have memories that will last forever."

Yes, Larry wants to visit Ireland, kiss the old Blarney Stone, and play a round of golf. His sights now, however, are on the near future — this year's 4th of July BBQ. The annual family BBQ was started in 1970 by his Dad, and with the exception of 1999 (when his Dad had a hip replacement), it has carried on rain or shine. He and Kevin orchestrate a day filled with great food, loads of laughter, and games of bocce, ladder golf, and corn hole. "To steal a famous line," Larry says, "It's a tradition unlike any other."

Tradition, family, hard work, good friends, and fun — these are the ingredients that have made Larry's life rich and fulfilling. He is eager for tomorrow to begin.

MARK KOBY

It's late afternoon. His work day is over at Shelter Enterprises. It's been a productive day, but now it's time to throw a few things together and head north to the old cabin at Speculator. Couple of the guys may already be there. They'll get the stove fired up, the booze flowing, and the checker and chess boards out. Mark's got his wine and a couple of bottles of whiskey, a little weed, and enough food to keep them nourished for the weekend. Couple more guys may be in tonight, and tomorrow, no question, they are going to love his pork tenderloins stuffed with sweet sausage, apples and onions.

For Mark, the rugged outdoors has always been his life. "I'm a pretty simple guy," he says, "I don't need a lot of shit, never did." Out of high school, he had aspirations of becoming an architect, but after one year at Delhi, he knew college was not for him: "I did get an A+ in Grateful Dead Concerts and a B- in after mid-night *Twilight Zone* episodes." Mark worked for a year as assistant manager at a Hess Station in Woodlawn and then took a job with Rick Cooper, a subcontractor for construction companies where he worked on house framing. Mark says that house framing allowed him to practice so many of his natural skills from drawing to the actual construction of the frames for the houses. "We worked like hell, and I loved it — probably did a hundred houses a year."

Mark then took a position with Homestead Builders in Scotia continuing much of the same work until he saw the opportunity to open his own cabinet shop — where he could be independent and exercise his own creativity. In his Scotia shop, he learned a lot from a master cabinet maker who worked with him — Frank Deltry. "This guy had hands the size of basketballs, but, man, did he have the skills." Mark ran his own business for 14 years until he got an offer from Jeff Meyers to buy the shop. Mark then went to work for Jeff who owns Shelter Enterprises in Cohoes, a company that specializes in building with Geofoam, lightweight fill material, which functions in multiple ways in construction. Mark takes a lot of pride in his work. He is especially proud of one building Shelter Enterprises played a role in con-structing — the Spring Street Salt Shed, a huge structure, supposedly an abstract representation of a salt grain, that houses road salt. This building Mark says, "really hits you when you come out of the Holland Tunnel." Working on that project was a high point of what Mark has done in the building and construction world.

Asked about any major plans Mark has for the future, he acknowledges that he does not have much of a bucket list. "I've done pretty much all I wanted to do. I will keep working hard, but I don't have a big wish list of things I still want to do." In a way Mark is a throwback to a simpler kind of life when essential needs were few and pleasures pretty simple. With lots of laughter mixed in. It has pretty much been this way from the beginning.

The first, longest, and best friend Mark ever had was Goober. The name Goober surfaced because at age three, Mark couldn't pronounce Rob Guzior's last name, so he called him Goober. "I still remember the day we met in January of 1969. My Mom was babysitting Goober who lived across the street. That day my father had on the Super Bowl game with Joe Namath and the New York Jets — I will never forget that game on the old black and white television my parents had." What made Goober and then later his friend Jeff Cleveland, whom he met through a mutual friend, so special is that each of his friends always had his back. Mark laughs when he recalls the night he and Jeff met at a local bar. "After a couple of beers and probably a couple of joints, we ended up going down to the IUE Hall in Schenectady and seeing the band "Slip Knot." (That night he also met Christine whom he would go on to marry twenty five years later.) Mark recalled that Jeff was looking for a roommate for a house he was renting. Mark gave it some thought and moved in a few days later. They had lots of good times together, and "I remember Jeff saved my ass a number of times when I was struggling."

The love of football that started with Joe Namath and the Jets continued in high school when Mark played for Gibbons: two years on the junior varsity and two years on the varsity. "We won three games on the JV under Coach Nicolella, and I think we even beat CBA. In two years on varsity football, we won one game." Mark laughs when he thinks about the lack of victories, but he still loved playing. "Of course, we were in the Big Ten, and there were some pretty good teams out there."

Asked about the leadership of Brother Moffett and Brother Flaherty, Principal and Vice-Principal during Mark's high school years, he commented, "Ahhh, I don't think they liked me very much, but I did get along with Brother Dead (Brother McLoughlin). He was cool. We would chat in the cafeteria when he was collecting his pennies." He also has fond memories of his religion teacher, Brother Miller. "He liked a lot of the music I liked and we would exchange albums — the Grateful Dead, Buffalo Springfields, Neil Young, Poco. He was kind of a mellow, friendly guy."

Mark's eyes light up when he talks about helping classmate Carl Stocker get his pig from Carl's mom's car into a classroom. Carl's mother had driven up from Cobleskill with Carl's pig named Bacon in the trunk of her car. Carl and Mark went out to the parking lot to meet her so that they could get Bacon, put him in a burlap bag, and carry him into Mr. O'Brien's English class. Carl presented first that day and spoke enthusiastically about Bacon, whom Carl had tied to the base of the podium with a short rope. When the presentation was over, Carl gave the room a touch of Lysol spray, and then he and Mark brought Bacon back to Mrs. Stockard who was waiting patiently in the car.

Another memorable occasion for Mark during his high school years occurred at Brant Lake. It was the senior retreat and the retreat team led by Father Joseph Busch had selected, as Mark recalls, an "old Victorian place" for the retreat. "But we had a crew — Heller, Wargo, Ferrari and a bunch of others who came armed with vodka, Jack Daniels, and smokes. As soon as the evening retreat work was done, we got to work with our stuff. A few hours passed, and then Father Busch on a check to see what we were up to discovered us, pretty much wasted. I had never seen him so pissed. He told us that the retreat was over, and that we were all going home at the crack of dawn. And for a starter, we were to call our parents and have them waiting at school for us — 6:30 in the morning."

Despite that night, Mark and Father Busch have maintained their friendship over the years even though they don't see each other often. "He is a class guy, and I still remember after the suicide of a classmate a couple of years after graduation, he sought me out fearing that I might get myself in trouble. A class guy."

Mark has taken the step to the altar twice: the first marriage to Tessa lasted ten years; the second to Christine lasted ten years. Even though each marriage ended, Mark has remained friendly with both women. About Christine, Mark says, "We seem to get along magnificently when we live separately."

When life is quiet and he has time, Mark loves to read. Among his favorite authors are John Sanford, Stewart Woods, and John Grisham. Mark is also politically astute and will not hesitate to let you know where he stands on issues. Mark loves dogs, and he recalls with special fondness a little grey terrier name Hammy who arrived about the same time as his second wife Christine and passed in 2018. Mark's new apartment in Cohoes is pet-friendly, and he is eager to adopt a new dog to share some good times.

When one thinks of characters in literature that Mark echoes, Randle Patrick McMurphy from *One Flew Over the Cuckoo's Nest* comes to mind, a gambling, brawling, game-playing character who is overflowing with life. As soon as McMurphy arrives on the hospital ward, the narrator notices something about him — his voice, his demeanor, his spirit of independence. Likewise when you meet Mark, you sense you are in the presence of a person of self-reliance, generosity, openness, and a sharp sense of the humorous absurdities of life. Soon, you discover that along with those qualities, you have a good and decent man, who is pretty much connected to the essential realities of life.

When he was five years old, Mark begged his father to take him deer hunting at the same site in Speculator that Mark visits today. His father did, and that togetherness began what was the most important relationship of Mark's formative years. Asked to speak about one moment that stands out in his life, Mark paused and then said, "the day my Dad died." When he was asked to say what made his Dad so special, Mark answered with one word — "Time." He paused for a moment and then said, "He always had time for me, whether it was a football game, a Scout meeting, a fishing trip, hunting. He was always there."

Mark Koby doesn't need much to enjoy each day, and he usually gives his best, whether at work or at play. After all, he says, "I'm a pretty simple guy. I don't need a lot of shit, never did."

KEVIN BARRY

"Certain moments are frozen in time." That's the way Kevin Barry describes moments that are touchstones on his journey, moments that illuminated, that transformed, or moments that crystalized an experience: the first two notes of a John Williams' score; the time on the Yankee Stadium scoreboard; the crack of a horse whip; a sentence — "Your Dad is so cool" —, the rhythm of a teacher's voice as the teacher corrects a Regents exam. These are moments that echo with meaning on the road Kevin Barry has traveled.

One of the moments occurred during Kevin's junior year in high school. Christmas season and Notre Dame-Bishop Gibbons had a space at the Mohawk Mall for Christmas wrapping. On a Saturday night, ND-BG students and parents were pitching in with the wrapping to help make a few dollars for the school. Kevin was there, but he was more interested in strolling around the mall than in wrapping. His father was at the table with a couple of other parents and students. On the Monday following, Nancy, one of the students at the wrapping table, said to Kevin in the hallway of school,"Your Dad is the coolest guy!" Kevin nodded but inside was taken back, saying to himself, "Wait, he is my Dad. How can someone who doesn't really know him say such a thing? How can she know that?" And then Kevin started thinking about his Dad and about how much his Dad loved people and was so generous sharing with others, and it began to hit him that Nancy had spoken the truth, had seen what up until this moment he had not seen clearly himself. "That was a moment when I started to become an adult."

Kevin at times tested the patience and tolerance of his parents, but as he puts it, "I told them the truth." As he was about to head out on a Friday night, his parents wondered what was going on. "Not much," Kevin would say, "we're just going up to the cemetery to hang out and drink a few beers." When he would tell his friends what he said to his parents, they were in disbelief. Most of them would lie and say that they were going to a game or a dance, but Kevin told the truth. His parents set a curfew though. "Be home before midnight." Kevin points out that he made the deadlines. "They gave me enough rope, but I never hanged myself. I knew that if I didn't make that deadline, I wasn't going out. I was usually home by 11:45."

A mark Kevin almost missed was a passing grade on the eleventh grade math Regents. He knew he was in dangerous waters, and so did his math teacher, Mr. Maguire. And so Kevin stayed every day after school preparing for the exam with Mr. Maguire. When the exam was over, Mr. Maguire directed Kevin to sit next to him for the correcting. "I was sailing along doing pretty well until we got to the word question.

It was a disaster. I had gotten totally lost. And as Mr. Maguire began to see what was going on, two things happened: he spoke to me and he used his pointer: 'You — WHACK — know — WHACK — better — WHACK — than — WHACK — this! WHACK. We — WHACK — went — WHACK — over — WHACK — this!! WHACK WHACK!!' I was about ready to say, 'Just fail me ' to avoid getting whacked any more.' But you know what, I passed and I wouldn't have made it without Mr. Maguire."

Sometimes the right teacher just happens to come along. In high school Kevin ran track for two years and played baseball for two years, but in his senior year when Kevin was a member of the bowling team he met an outstanding coach. Tom Donato, the son of the legendary Joe Donato, perhaps the best bowler ever from the area, was Kevin's coach. "He was the coolest guy, and he knew so much about bowling. It was a privilege to have him as my coach." The knowledge and spirit he gained from Coach Donato kept Kevin active in the game as he continued to bowl for over 25 years, often with his father.

Kevin inherited his love of the Yankees from his father, and speaks with emotion and joy of two moments that he shared with his Dad. In the final game of the 1996 World Series, they watched Mark Lemke's foul ball off the bat of John Wetteland's pitch being caught by Charlie Hays to end the game, the first World Series victory for the Yankees since 1978. And then later seeing the panoramic photograph of Wade Boggs with the official Yankee clock at 10:56 in the background and in the picture the tiny figures of Kevin and his Dad in the crowd. Finally being with his Dad in maybe the most fitting place of all — the final game in the old Yankee Stadium in 2008, the last Yankee game Kevin's father ever saw in person.

Kevin's passion about life is intense, and there are moments when his eyes are open wide and he is at fever pitch.

Listen to him talk about the movie *Jaws*. "I was too young when it opened in 1975, but in 1978, I saw it as a ten-year-old. I remember the day vividly. I wore a Yankee hat which had a mesh in the back. Once John Williams struck the first two notes of the theme for the shark, I whipped my hat around and watched the movie through the mesh of my hat." For Kevin, *Jaws* ranks at the very top of his all-time favorite films. If you listen to him speak about Quint's monologue recounting the doomed fate of the USS Indianapolis, you will be held almost as much as the viewers were held by the monologue itself. "The scene with Quint is perfection. It is probably the greatest film monologue ever."

Among books Kevin is passionate about are three of his favorites: *Not a Good Day to Die* by Sean Naylor. "I have read it twice and it may be the first book I will read three times. Amazing story — the highest altitude the U.S. Military ever fought at — over 10,000 feet above sea level; *Bruce Dickinson: What Does This Button Do. An Autobiography.* Bruce is the lead singer of Iron Maiden. It's his story of growing up in England and singing in one of heavy metals's biggest bands. One of the wild things is that he becomes a commercial airline pilot and flies his band, crew, and gear around the world. Also he overcomes oral cancer and continues to sing; *LA Son* by Roy Choi, the story of a great chef who left his five-star restaurant to open a food truck in LA. Great story."

Thanks to the influence of his older brother Larry, Kevin got into music early. "REO Speedwagon, Queen, Ozzy Osborne, AC-DC — hard rock and metal were sort of a blueprint for my life." He talks about how his musical tastes evolved — I appreciate Stevie R. Vaughan, BB King, the Blues, but so much of my early life was shaped by metal and hard rock." One song by Guns and Roses has very special meaning — "Sweet Child O' Mine." I love this song that I first heard in my teenage years, and now that I have a daughter it has taken on even more meaning.

"Sierra is amazing," Kevin says. Now in her freshmen year at SUNY Oswego, he recalls one of those moments that served as a revelation to him about his daughter. At the age of 14, Sierra was helping out at a horse farm. On this particular day, Kevin drove her out to the farm so that she could exercise a horse. After bringing the horse out of the barn, Sierra stood back and cracked her whip. "I watched her with the horse. She cracked the whip, the horse started running. She cracked the whip, the horse stopped. She cracked the whip, the horse started up. I was amazed. They were communicating." Sierra has always loved horses, from the time Kevin had ponies brought to her birthday parties. In recent years she has become a skilled equestrian and spends much of her free time, especially during COVID, tending to horses at a local farm. And next to Kevin, there is no greater pal to Kevin's dog Cody than Sierra.

COVID also played a major role in Kevin's life for two reasons: his job and his health. After earning two degrees at HVCC, one in liberal arts, one in medical imaging, Kevin worked at Albany Medical Center from 1992 until 2000, followed by seven years at St. Clare's and ten more years when they merged with Ellis. In 2017 he took a position with Abbott, a job which involved instructing doctors about company products for surgical procedures. He was pleased with the work and felt that he played a meaningful role. COVID slowed everything down — elective procedures were put off and vendors were kept out. It was in the slow-down period that his old boss suggested that he interview with a new company called Shock Wave Medical. He was impressed and took a position as a clinical specialist who does inservice with doctors and staff on the latest vascular devices. "Shock Wave is on the cutting edge of product innovation, and I am happy to be part of it."

In early 2020, Kevin's weight had reached an all-time high, and a moment on a cruise with his brother and daughter was an eye-opener. The ride he wanted to go on had a 250 weight maximum, and although he was allowed to take the ride even though he was slightly over, he knew something had to be done. COVID had arrived and Kevin took full advantage by putting in an hour a day on the treadmill and changing his diet dramatically, concentrating on healthy foods and focusing on one major meal a day. Within six months, he had lost over 50 pounds. "COVID gave me time to exercise and time to rethink my diet. It payed off."

During COVID Kevin had begun to watch shows that two years prior he couldn't have imagined himself watching — cooking shows. He began to develop his culinary skills significantly, sometimes treating the family — his daughter, Mom, Larry and his girlfriend Jackie and whoever else wanted to join him — to dinner on a Sunday night with surf and turf or a good old-fashioned stew. In many ways for Kevin, the COVID year was a good year.

In general, Kevin is pretty happy these days. He has the solid support of family and friends, and maintains a good relationship with his former spouse Tamara, who stopped in recently to help him with his taxes. As summer approaches, he will tune up his golf clubs and get ready for League play at Van Patten Golf Course. On his long-range bucket list is playing a round at Pebble Beach. He still has a few places he would like to visit, Ireland at the top of the list and then maybe New Zealand. And he has his great buddy, his dog Cody. Nothing is better than an evening with a good movie on and Sierra and Cody relaxing with him after a good meal that he prepared. These are the simple but beautiful moments Kevin treasures.

RACHEL REBANAL DELGADO

There are moments in life that serve to help us see the path ahead; and then there are moments that test the strength and resolve in our character. One vital moment of insight came for Rachel Rebanal Delgado during the summer after her sophomore year at Seton Hall University when she worked at St. Clare's Hospital Day Care. In the summer program, she found joy working with children, and she decided that she would shift her major from business to education. She would become a teacher. The second moment came when she made the decision right after graduating from Seton Hall to accept a teaching job in a tough neighborhood in East Orange, New Jersey, when she knew that her parents had safety concerns about this move and preferred that she come home and pursue a master's degree. Her decision to become a teacher, Rachel will attest, was the right one;

her decision to start teaching in a very challenging environ-ment turned out to be a good one too.

Rachel's foundation was strong, growing up in a close-ly-knit family with two older brothers and a younger sister. Her father was a surgeon and her mother a nurse. Both par-ents put a top priority on Catholic education, and all four of the children went through elementary, high school, and col-lege at Catholic schools. Her parents also stressed the value of hard work with her Dad's mantra being, "Anything worth doing is worth doing well." Rachel's three siblings followed in their parents' footsteps by pursuing careers in the biomedi-cal fields. Rachel took a different path and choose the world of education.

Her father was concerned when Rachel told him that she wanted to change her major from business to education, after her summer working at St. Clare's. A business school promised a job and security, whereas an education degree was less certain. But Rachel's heart and passion had turned toward education. She changed her program at Seton Hall from a business major to an elementary education/English literature co-major. The program at the Hall was thorough and rigorous and prepared her well for the teaching world. "I had four internships and a semester of student teaching — I probably had 100 hours in placements in three different semesters. I had one in a Catholic school, one in an urban public school, one in a suburban public school, and one in a Montessori school. I selected the urban public school for my student teaching since I had a good relationship with my cooperating teacher and felt I could learn so much there."

At J. Garfield Jackson Sr. Academy in East Orange, New Jersey, Rachel did her student teaching. Right after that teach-ing, Rachel, who graduated from Seton Hall in May of 2001, took a position as an interim reading teacher to finish out the academic year and then accepted a position that fall to teach second graders. East Orange, New Jersey, is a tough city with its fair share of crime and drugs, but Rachel was determined to teach at J. Garfield. She began that fall with a class of 25 second graders, and a bouquet of flowers that arrived from her parents during the first week. "My cooperating teacher (and later teaching partner) and her grade-level colleague during my internship were phenomenal." They showed Rachel how the classroom could be infused with passion, how a teacher could have high expectations for young learners, and how to command respect. "My cooperating teacher took a lot of time to sit with me and reflect on my lessons and students. She was real with me about the profession and modeled a lot of the things education courses do not get into such as classroom management.... I learned so much during my time there."

One day Rachel's parents showed up after school and spent time in her classroom, listening to Rachel talk about her work. They now understood much more clearly that their daughter was passionate about the profession of teaching, and they were impressed by her commitment and dedication. She could see in their eyes that they were proud of their daughter.

Rachel's teaching journey would become more challenging. After three years at J. Garfield, she took a position at Washington Academy in Cedar Grove, NJ, a private K-12 school for students with special needs. Many of the students had behavioral disorders and were emotionally disturbed. Rachel team-taught with two special education teachers in a classroom with 10-12 students, grades 4-6. The students received individual and group counseling daily and because of this counseling and the student teacher ratio, they were better able to access the learning material. The team support was vital because the emotional and physical intensity was often very high. "It was here that I realized that all children, not just those with IEP's, have individual goals, develop at different rates, and need personal attention and relationships with their teacher."

While Rachel was teaching at Washington Academy, she was also studying at night for her Master's in Instruction and Curriculum at Kean University. Then on a trip to Boston with friends in the summer of 2004, she reconnected with a high school classmate — Kito Delgado. They met again at a birthday party that winter and began dating shortly after.

Kito had earned a business degree from Northeastern and a year after they had begun dating took a job in Manhattan in the insurance industry. In 2009, Rachel and Kito married. After she finished the 2009-10 academic year at Washington Academy, Rachel and Kito moved back to the Capital District where she began her work on her New York teaching certification. During this period, she was a support teacher in North Colonie three days a week and subbed two days a week. In 2011, she was hired as a fifth grade teacher at Glen-Worden Elementary School in Scotia-Glenville where she worked until 2019. Her most recent teaching position since the fall of 2019 has been in the Shenendehowa School District.

Given the pandemic, this past year has been a challenge and a victory of sorts for Rachel. When the department chair asked for one of the teaching team members to take over the remote learning for the year, no one volunteered. She gave Kito a quick call to see what he thought, and he told her absolutely yes. Everything fell into place. It didn't take her long to learn the essentials of teaching the virtual program, and Melina, their daughter, who was in first grade, was able to stay at home for two months with her father who was working from home. Rachel's hours of virtual teaching run from 8:30 in the morning until 1:30 with planning time before and after. Despite all the limitations of virtual teaching, Rachel still finds that she loves working with her kids.

Rachel has fond memories of her own years as a student, "I would go back at any time — it was fun." There are friendships she made in high school — Meg, Zulvey, Mike, and Lucas — that are still strong. She holds memories that are vivid. One, in particular, centered on a guided meditation exercise in the chapel led by her religion teacher, Sister Jeanne Fielder. The students were asked to close their eyes and picture Jesus. As Sister continued to lead them in the meditation, Rachel felt herself getting very emotional and totally immersed in visualizing Jesus. Later in the classroom, she was telling Sister Jeanne how powerful the experience was for her when her friend Mike Dickerson said, "How soon can she enter the order, Sister?" Another memorable time in high school was the trip to Spain led by Spanish teacher, Melanie Anchukaitis. "Oh my gosh, I loved the trip and it made me want to travel. One of the really cool things is that we were able to go off on our own a few times."

Travel also opened Rachel's eyes to other worlds when she journeyed with her family to visit their ancestral home and their relatives in the Philippines. "We visited sections that were so poverty-stricken, and I saw how hard it was for people." Seeing the dire state of so many people, she realized how fortunate she was to live the life she has lived. Rachel thanks God for the opportunities she was given.

Her spirit is fully alive when there is music. "I am a HUGE 90's, early 2000s R&B and Hip Hop fan." Among her favorites are New Edition, Lauryn Hill, and Mary J. Blige. Rachel and Kito always have music playing, and sometimes they break into dance. "I love to sing, especially when I'm happy." One song that Rachel loves to dance and sing to is "No Letting Go" by Wayne Wonder. That is her happy song: "No letting go No holding back / No Holding Back No / When I'm with you it's all of that / All of that." Music to her also speaks of moments in time: "One album that brings me to a transformative and memorable time — Sept. 2001; first apartment, first job, 9-11, is Jay-z's *The Blueprint*. The first song on that album, "The Ruler's Back," — the build up and the horns, can transport me back to that crazy time."

In her busy schedule as teacher, wife, and mom, Rachel still tries to find time to read: whether it's a best seller like *Where the Crawdads Sing* or the latest Emily Giffin novel or a reread of a favorite classic like *Wuthering Heights* or Morrison's *Song of Solomon*. When time is tight, she will pick up her anthology from college and read a few poems by her favorite poets, William Wordsworth and William Blake. Of course, her evenings never conclude without reading a bedtime story to her daughter Melina. And often giving Melina one of her favorite quotes from Emerson, "Be silly, be honest, be kind."

What keeps Rachel so positive about her life? She would say that a large part of it is her Faith, instilled and nurtured by her parents at home and one that she and Kito now share with their daughter. "Every day begins with prayer," Rachel says. She is also very happy in her marriage. "Kito has been so good for me. He's realistic. He challenges me and helps me to see my life more clearly." What Rachel has come to appreciate about Kito is that he is a great listener. "Friends say they leave almost every discussion having learned something because of Kito's angle of vision." According to Rachel, Kito's passion is helping others elevate and grow. One of his special strengths is working with young athletes, showing them how to best navigate the complicated world of recruiting and maintaining the balance of sports and academics.

Praying, working hard, celebrating family and being open to the music of life — these are some of the essentials that make Rachel Rebanal Delgado such an outstanding teacher and such a positive person.

IMANI EICHELBERGER

When Imani and her brother Clayton were very young, their mother would stand them in front of the mirror, and they would say, "I know I am somebody and I am a force to be reckoned with." Today, Dr. Imani Eichelberger is a pediatrician who works at Hampton Roads Pediatrics in Norfolk, Virginia; Clayton is an attorney who works for the New York State Senate.

From her earliest memories, Imani wanted to be a pediatrician, with a brief interlude spent thinking about the profession of teaching. "My parents instilled in us the idea of pursuing what we were passionate about, what we wanted to do." The family pediatrician was a role model for Imani. "Dr. Luthera was enthusiastic about her work, and she seemed to love being a pediatrician." Imani also had an early experience with the healing work of doctors when she caught her hand at home in the lever of a La Z Boy chair causing an injury that required serious attention. Dr. Lynch, a plastic surgeon, dealt with the injury, and as Imani recalls, "He was so nice he even let me help with the sutures."

Medical school was her goal, and Imani knew that it was a major educational commitment, but she had started well with the support of her parents, and there were other strong supports in the family. A major inspiration instilling the value of education was Imani's grandfather, Alfred Hunter. He worked at GE for fifty years, and though he never went to college, he always emphasized that "with an education, you can go anywhere." It was his Mom, Grace Moss Hunter, who attended Hampton Institute in the early 1900's before it became Hampton University. Both Imani (2011) and her brother (2009) are graduates of Hampton University.

In her pre-medical program at Hampton, Imani had a strong taste of the demands of the program. She recalled that in one semester during junior year, her day started with class at 9 a.m. and then with other classes, labs, and a MCAT prep class, her day ended at 9 p.m. She persevered and after graduating from Hampton, she entered Eastern Virginia Medical School in Norfolk, VA. After the rigors of in-class book work for the first two years, she had the chance to work in hospitals, which she loved. She did, however, have a moment which tested her and revealed that she had more support than she realized. On the second major step required for program certification, she didn't meet the necessary score. Though she felt fear and doubt, she found the time and space for a prep course. It was at this moment that she felt the love of her father. On his own, Earl went through the entire prep program and sectioned it off by topic. Then he went through the videos and made a poster size calendar that laid out the schedule for study each day with the program. "He knew how he could best help me, and I followed his study calendar exactly and ended up reaching the necessary score. By doing what he did, he made me feel that it was doable. I was so grateful."

Her residency in pediatrics was at Children's Hospital of the King's Daughters in Norfolk. Attending to the needs of children gave Imani the opportunity to encourage young people to follow their dreams — that they too could become a doctor or lawyer or whatever they desired. In a real way, she was emulating what was done for her by her parents. During her residency program, Imani also had the opportunity to spend a month working with young people in India and two weeks with the young in Haiti. These experiences were very meaningful and planted seeds in her for future travel.

On July 10, 2019, Imani's father, Earl, died. He had been suffering from Crohn's disease when things took a turn for the worse. For Imani, a major source of influence was gone. Educated at LeMoyne with a master's in social work from Syracuse, Earl had worked a number of years at the New York State Division of Youth, followed by 14 years with the NYS Parole Board. "It was hard work with long hours, especially with the Parole Board. Often he left early on Monday and didn't return until the end of the week." When Imani and Clayton started moving into middle school, Earl left his job at the Parole Board and took a position with the New York State Catholic Conference. "He really wanted to be around for Clayton and me to support us in our school activities." In Imani's eyes, her father in his own quiet way never stopped encouraging her and her brother to do their best in whatever they did. "One thing about my Father's death was that it caused me to slow down and look at life and try to appreciate each moment."

The pandemic of the last year has also had its lessons for Imani, "Although I have been frustrated at times with those in our community who refuse to get on board with the most simple requests — wear a mask, for example — I have seen so many good signs of neighbors reaching out to neighbors, helping those most in need in the community." Imani has seen people becoming aware of what really mattered, the importance of family and friendships, and what it means to lose someone.

After the death of her Dad, Imani made an extra effort to spend more time with her Mom, Carla, her best friend in so many ways, which included taking a cruise together. Before becoming a teacher, Carla had worked for the New York State Legislature where she met Earl. Once the two kids were in Guilderland Elementary School, Carla began teaching there as an assistant and followed that year with teaching positions at St. Patrick's in Troy, St. Casimir's in Albany for a long stretch, and then St. Kateri's in Schenectady. When Imani was asked what her Mom's best quality is, she offered one word — "kindness. She will go out of her way to do something kind for people."

In her senior research paper for Honors English, Imani did a study of Alice Walker's *The Color Purple,* the story of one young woman's long journey of self discovery and self realization. When Imani stood in front of the audience at St. John the Evangelist Church to give her high school's salutatorian address, she did not lack for self-confidence. Supported and inspired by her parents all along, she had often practiced public speaking, and her voice was strong and clear. About to head off for a pre-med program at Hampton University, she was looking back with a smile at four strong and enjoyable years of high school.

Notre Dame-Bishop Gibbons was a good experience for Imani, even when a scheduling problem turned out at first to be an issue but ended up being a positive for her. Because her math program from her previous school had not included a required course that would allow her to be in an honors schedule across the board, she was assigned one non-honors class — math. That class turned out to be an enjoyable experience for Imani. The class tended to be on the rowdy side, but, in Imani's eyes, they were an education too. "And when we had Mr. Maguire, he made math so easy to understand. I was learning and having lots of laughs too."

"I played volleyball and got talked into going out for track and field," Imani says with a smile. Friends encouraged her. "Tina and Kayleigh told me 'to just do it. You don't have to do much, just hang out.'" Imani threw the discus and shot. At practice she would loft the discus a few times and then relax a bit. "One day Coach Broderick told us to go on this running route, and we started out but after a couple of blocks we stopped and said to each other, 'We didn't join track and field to run and then burst into laughter.'"

Maybe Imani's easy and joyful laugh is one of the best markers of her equanimity. "What's meant to be will be," is a favorite quotation of hers, and she falls back on this thought when life seems to get too much. She has developed patterns that help give her balance and peace in her life. "On my day off, I often visit a favorite bake shop in town and enjoy a slice of freshly baked bread with tea. I love to sit there and read and just be. I also love going out to the beach and just relaxing near the water." She admits that sometimes she just stays home and binge watches a few shows on Netflix. When Imani gets a little extra time, she drives north to Albany and visits her Mom. She also loves seeing her niece Corina who is now three and "a blast to spend time with. She is feisty, hilarious, and such a sweet lovable girl." Sometimes she and her brother meet for dinner. "It's always good to be with Clayton and get caught up on what he's doing. He is very thoughtful. He can sum up things too in a humorous and concise way. When I used to worry about dating, he would say, 'Imani, don't waste your time.' I would laugh. What he was saying in his own succinct way was that things will work out. Someone will come along. In a way, Clayton is a lot like my dad."

Music has always had a special place in Imani's soul. "I like lots of music, but Gospel music has a special place for me. I was in a Gospel choir from 4th through 9th grades. Our church had people from West Indies and Africa and you could really get into the music. On hard days, it would make you feel uplifted. I still look for good Gospel music wherever I am." One of Imani's favorite Gospel singers is Smokie Norful whose song "I Need You Now" is one of her favorites:

"I need you to make a way / As you have done so many times before / Through window or an open door / I stretch my hands to thee / Come rescue me / I need you right away."

After her father's death, Imani says, "I was going through the motions, and then I met Victor through online dating in June of 2020." Imani appreciates Victor's patience and gentle spirit. "He helped me to begin to enjoy life again, and our relationship is good." One thing Victor has shared with Imani is his love of fishing. "The first time we went out on the ocean, I reeled in 14 or 15 fish. We were actually getting really competitive. It was so much fun." Victor is also an excellent cook and he is always trying new dishes. "His New Orleans pasta with homemade alfredo sauce is so good."

Under Imani's picture in her high school yearbook is this quotation by Marianne Williamson, "Our deepest fear is not that we are inadequate. Our deepest fear is that we are powerful beyond measure." When asked about the truth of this statement today, Imani admitted that "deepest fear" in the second sentence could be changed to "greatest strength." She now has reached a point where she knows that with her skill and knowledge, she can accomplish so much. No question, her Mom made a strong impression with the mirror and the words. Dr. Imani Eichelberger is proof.

TINA JONES

In *The Shawshank Redemption,* Andy Dufresne says, "Remember, Red, hope is a good thing, maybe the best of things, and no good thing ever dies." Hope is one of the qualities that marks Tina Jones. Wherever she has been, Tina has manifested a hopeful spirit, sharing with others and serving others. Tina is one of those souls that lifts others up and gives them the sense that the journey is worthwhile.

In talking about her life, Tina speaks with verve and thoughtfulness, remembering what mattered even back when the contours of her life were still undefined. Speaking about graduation from high school, Tina recalls that she "had the sense that a gorgeous chapter in her life was coming to an end." So many fond memories of moments and friendships — "Jordan, Angie, Amber, Lauren, Kaileigh, Katie, John, Dej — very happy time ... many of my friends then are still my friends today." She throws her head back and laughs at memories of math teacher Mr. Maguire. "We had a love/shut the hell up relationship." Totally exasperated with her, he would say, "You're so smart but you act like such a dumb ass." She remembers with pride pouring her heart and soul into her forty page journal on Toni Morrison's *Song of Solomon* and earning an A from Mr. O'Brien. She smiles when she thinks of her efforts and attempts in volleyball and track. "I wasn't the greatest athlete, but I enjoyed getting out and participating."

In volleyball, Tina loved her chats with Coach Baseel, and she is thrilled that they remain good friends today. She remembers hiding with Kaileigh in the back of the stage during rehearsals so that they could listen to one of her favorite classmates, Jonathan Wood, sing musical numbers from *West Side Story* and *My Fair Lady*.

"I love all kinds of music," Tina says. In her high school years, music turned into a source of comfort and inspiration. "Kate Miller-Heike's 'Caught in the Crowd' has major high school vibes. I feel like I've been all of these people. I mean, I think we all have. To someone."

She throws back her head in laughter when she thinks of traveling during those years with her Mom and sister Abby to Oneonta with the tunes playing. "I loved listening to Joni Mitchell, Annie Lenox, Sheryl Crow, Fleetwood Mac, and Alanis Morissette." Tina also reminisces about how she, Abby, and their Pop had their own genre called "Green Truck Music" which translated into "feel good fun dad rock with a twang." Asked to pick one artist that rates at the top of her list, Tina says, "Overall, I think I'd have to say Van Morrison —- I just feel understood and connected and timeless when I listen to him. His song 'Sweet Thing" reminds me of my dear friend, Jon Wood." One album that Tina cites as crucial was Neil Young's "Live at Massey Hall," which she had received as a gift after high school from Mr. O'Brien who was a Young devotee. "I adore that album. I listened to it 'ad nauseum,' and it definitely helped me navigate through some uncharted territories." Tina even used the song "On the Way Home" from the album as the subject of a final paper for one of her college writing classes. Three songs she has listened to over and over: "Same Drugs" by Chance the Rapper, "The Minstrel's Prayer" by Cartel, and "Yesterday" by Atmosphere. "Especially at times when I needed strength or needed to feel sane or understood, these songs made a difference. They all sing about a longing, and it all feels so familiar. And then — there's hope: We have a song."

No question, music has spoken and continues to speak to Tina's soul. Wherever Tina has been, she has created her own song, one measured by her commitment, her openness, and a joy that radiates to others. After completing her degree in psychology at Siena College in 2011, Tina took a full time position as a waitperson at the Waters Edge Lighthouse, continuing work in the restaurant industry she had worked in since high school. At times she questioned her choice of work when so many of her friends from college had so-called "real jobs," but for Tina the work in this setting turned out to be vital for her own growth, and, she adds, "just about as real as it gets." She speaks of those years with passion. "In many ways I feel like I grew up there — grew into an adult. I learned a lot. I learned a lot about people and a lot about myself. I worked very hard, and I made a lot of money there. Pat Popolizio, the owner, kept a person honest, let me tell you, and I learned a supreme work ethic, for which I am forever grateful. I met people who left huge and lasting impacts on me. People at the Lighthouse stood by me during some of the worst moments and times of my entire life."

What also added to Tina's belief in herself through those years was the strong support of her parents, "My mom told me she was proud of her daughters who were making an honest living, learning real life and business skills, and making good money in the restaurant industry. My dad had always been in the industry since he was a young boy washing dishes while a student at Notre Dame-Bishop Gibbons and was happy we were seeing that world first hand."

A fortuitous event turned Tina's life in a new direction in February of 2015. "After seeing an ad for the Wellness School of Massage Therapy in Albany, I stopped into the Wellness Center, filled out an application and went on a tour. It just felt right." She had always loved massage and its healing and calming powers, so it was a world that seemed natural and right. She graduated from the Center in April 2016, got her New York State License that October and her nationally recognized license shortly after. After working as a massage therapist at a spa in a casino and then independently for a period, Tina accepted a position in June of 2018 with Spa Mirbeau in Albany, where she felt at home almost immediately. She was determined to be outstanding at what she did and so immediately began to expand her skill set. She took a number of courses in what is known as Myofascial Release, the John Barnes Approach, a hands-on modality that involves gentle, sustained pressure into the restrictions of the myofascial connective tissues in order to create space, eliminate pain, and restore motion to the body. "Myofascial Release," Tina says, "is the bodywork modality that I practice with great passion."

Recently Tina has become an instructor for Myofascial Release at the Center for Natural Wellness. "I get to help spark the passion in others."

Tina is the first to admit that taking up massage therapy was essential to her in a larger sense. "The tribe of ladies I met in massage school has added immeasurable joy and sisterhood to my life." Those she shared the journey with during and after massage school are all working toward the same goals of minimizing the pain for living beings. As Tina puts it, "Everyone needs bodywork. Everyone deserves body work. Everyone needs and deserves a safe touch and a safe space." Another really special meaning that has emerged for Tina is that in her massage work, she sees classmates, teachers, and parents from her high school days. It's a great example of the idea of staying connected and caring for those you know.

Tina is a vegan. This step on her journey, shared with her sister Abby, has been very positive for her. "Abby is a steadfast and strong-willed, gentle person who is a wonderful support." The process of becoming vegan, however, was not a quick one for Tina. "It was a year long transition from pescatarian to vegetarian to vegan." Tina believes that it was the right path for her to take, but she knows that "it has to happen when people are ready." She is thrilled that many of her family members and friends are vegan, and she says, "along with pursuing a career in massage, it was one of the best decisions I ever made."

At this point on her journey, Tina feels good about her life. She has a solid relationship with her partner Zach who is also a massage therapist. Zach came into Tina's life at a good time. "My personal life had gotten a bit on the wild side, and Zach helped to ground me. In many ways, he has helped to bring a calmness and steadiness into my life. I appreciate him." One cool thing for Tina is that Zach also works at Spa Mirabeau and "we even get to do an occasional couples massage together." Zach also brought his cat named Scooter into the relationship, and Tina holds nothing back when she says, "I'm absolutely in love with Scooter."

Though Tina knows that her life has become marked with purpose and good relationships, there is a wanderlust that stirs in her. She has traveled to eleven countries, sometimes alone, and has planned a trip around the world, once the journey is COVID-cleared.

Tina's ebullient spirit has always been marked by hope. As her journey has continued, Tina has in her own unique way arrived at the idea expressed by Ralph Waldo Emerson in the quotation under her picture in her high school yearbook: "Do not go where the path may lead. Go instead where there is no path and leave a trail." Tina Jones — trail blazer, healer, and believer in the power of hope.

With My Younger Brother

My brother Leo and my sister Rosemary are a number of years older than my brother John and I. It's as if they were one generation and the two of us were another. A number of the moments John and I shared I have spoken about in my book *Keys on the Road*, a retrospective about growing up in the village of Raymertown. Certain other moments I have carried with me and are part of the timeless markings in my soul. As I move onward, they move onward with me. One has to due with black raspberry pies.

First Moment: After the funeral service for my mother, our immediate family had traveled out to what we fondly call "The Ranch," a house built on a piece of property that was the land my mother and her brothers grew up on. The land had been purchased eventually by my brother Leo from the family. On this day we gathered and reminisced about my mother and the life she had led. It was a sad day in some ways, but positive in the sense that we shared so many good memories about Mom. When Debbie and I got home late that afternoon, I noticed that the raspberry bushes adjacent to the garage were rich with berries — for whatever reason, I had been oblivious to them prior to this moment. I looked at Debbie, and she smiled and said, "Yes, I will make a black raspberry pie." I filled almost two pots with berries, and from those she made one large pie and one small pie. That moment, kind of a miracle really — a gift from my mother, brought back our history and the role Mom played in creating our world.

"PRETTY GOOD"

On Saturday mornings
when we were kids
my mother would hand us
each a pot.
Mine might have been a bit larger
than John's -- I was a little older
and bigger.
Off we went
across Route 7
disappearing into the woods
of a neighboring farmer
where we would find
a thick growth of black raspberry bushes.
How did my mother know they were there?
To my knowledge neither she
nor my father ever crossed
the highway of Route 7.
The berries seemed to say,
"We have been waiting for you."
It's hard to describe

the berry picking
but time seemed to almost stop.
So quiet with faint rustling and brushing
as John's white tee-shirt
flickered in the bushes
and our fingers rolled the berries
into our pots.
The heat of the day slid in
bringing a haze to the air
buzzing and droning
my brother occasionally
slapping at a mosquito
a car humming by on Route 7
a reminder that though
we had disappeared
we were not far from home.
The pots would fill
and with purple fingers
and lips like clowns
we would nod
and turn towards home.
The highway —
Once crossing this highway
my brother slipped
losing half his berries —
In the afternoons
John and I would disappear
into the many summer
games of childhood
while my mother went to work.
On those nights

we couldn't wait
for dinner to conclude
with the best dessert
ever.
My father would say,
"Pretty good, huh."
I'd nod and say, "Yeah, Dad.
Pretty good"
Mom's Black Raspberry Pie.

Second Moment: When yearly celebrations arrive in a small town, you do what you can to make your statement. John and I made our statement, witnessed perhaps by no one else or maybe someone passing by at midnight on Route 7 through the village of Raymertown. To this day, if we remember, we work the light switch at midnight on New Year's.

LIGHTING THE YEAR
(An O'Brien tradition)

Long ago on New Year's Eve
In a village not too far away
Two young lads gathered their wits
To offer the world what they had to say.

'Twas a deed they thought so very cool
With their Mom and Dad off into sleep
They hoped to make the world a bit brighter
With just a small gesture, not really too deep.

With John in the kitchen
And Paul at the living room door
Each looked at the dining room clock
And waited a few seconds more.

As the clock reached the exact moment of twelve
Their hands went right to the wall
Up and down on the switch by the doors
Creating a dance of new light — for all.

I talked to my brother today
Far away in Boston's fair town
He's ready to go at the moment of twelve
He in Boston, me in Nisky — no fooling around.

Third Moment. Onward to the next generation as the world of brothers grows more complex when it becomes intertwined in the world of father, son, and uncle.

IT AIN'T OVER YET

"A dollar the Knicks win," I say exuding confidence and why not, the Knicks lead the conference finals two games to zero.

"No way," says my nephew Eamon, laughing as he spins a basketball in his left hand and then leans forward on the sofa to slap me five.

"Hey, Dad, Uncle Paul, how about shooting a few before the game starts. Come on, I'll take you two on."

John looks at me from his Lazy-Boy and gives me a slow grin and his famous eyebrow lift as if to say, "You're getting pretty good, boy, but it may be time for the two of us to put things into perspective."

The court itself is well-lit by a couple of spotlights, and the basketball backboard and rim on the edge of a smooth black-topped driveway is located to the left of the garage entrance. It's the type of court my brother and I wish we could have had as kids instead of the hoop over the garage door, with a lethal rut at its base that the garage door slid along in, and a slanted court that was composed of an uneven combination of grass, dirt, and blacktop. But we were good on that court — knew all the angles, the odd bounces on the choppy blacktop, the slope of the ground on the left side of the court, the softness of the wooden backboard that held the hoop. If the basketball bounced against the open garage door on the left, it was still in play — that was a beauty. Once, having clearly established the ground rules of our court, John and I defeated two friends from college who had played high school hoop. Neither one of us had played organized ball, but we sure knew what home court advantage was.

My first three warmup shots don't even touch the rim; my fourth shot floats weakly under the backboard and lands in a shrub a few feet past the court. "Nice shot, Uncle Paul," says my nephew as he drops a twelve foot jumper. "Hey, guys," he says, "first one to 21?" I look at John, who smiles, and I say, "Let's make it 15 — probably about it for me."

Barely has Eamon said, "Okay, let's go. My out," than he dribbles by me and scores with a layup. Though he's only in sixth grade, he's been playing organized ball for two years and it shows. Even in his bedroom decor: the room is adorned with Michael Jordan posters, enormous and spectacular dunks everywhere you look. I had seen Eamon play in a game a month or so earlier, and though only an armchair authority on hoop, I was impressed by his cool ball-handling skills as he brought the ball up court and was able to spot the open man often leading to a score. Fortunately, John has also played on this "home" court a number of times and has a shot that still drops in the old bucket.

"Yes!" John says as I make the third of three attempts right underneath. Thank God for my eight inch height advantage. But then Eamon steals an errant pass and proceeds to make three in a row closing within one of us. Each time Eamon scores, John glances at me and lifts the eyebrows. The fact that I have not played any basketball in five years — and that was only a few shots after school in the high school gym where I teach — is brutally apparent. Parchment dominates the inside of my mouth. I'm out of breath and desperately in need of a timeout. "Come on, push yourself, Paulie," I say to myself. "Score."

"I'm behind by one —12 to 11 — Let's do it," Eamon says as coolly as if he just started this game.

John gives me a breather by hitting two quick ones; then presses Eamon hard and manages to steal the ball which he lobs to me underneath, and I manage to somehow toss the winner in. It's over, and I stagger over to the stone wall near the front of the house.

"HORSE is next," Eamon says.

"Oh my God," I groan to myself, as I push myself up from the wall. In the old days, the game was OUT, and when it ended too suddenly — OUTS. I guess with HORSE I have an additional chance.

"No fancy shots," I say.

"Un huh," says Eamon with a smile and starts with a left-handed layup which I don't even come close to making, thus earning my H. With a series of shots off twisting, spinning moves, long jumpers, and Michael Jordan fade-aways, I'm HORSE in about four minutes. I have one chance to start over if I can hit a long shot from behind the stone wall (home court rules). My ball drops below the backboard — not even close. John manages to hang in for two more shots, and then he succumbs to a shot from three point land.

"Okay, Uncle Paul, you're next. One on one."

I look over at my nephew and then at my brother who gives me the left eyebrow lift, and then I push myself up from the wall I have collapsed on. "My God," I say to myself. "This is one of the moments you read about. The old man (nearly fifty) being challenged by the youngster." I think back to a recent story told by another nephew Dan, now in his mid-30's, about being challenged one night at the Y by a high school student. He died about three times on his way to a two point victory, but the near-deaths he kept well hidden. After his final shot had dropped through the hoop for the victory, he said to the high schooler, "And that, youngster, is how the game is played." I loved that line.

I am not ready to die, but I'm not ready to lose, not yet. I'm almost forty years older than this kid — there's got to be a way. My mind leaps to Colin, my brother-in-law, and the way he would score on us when we were kids. Though we had our home court advantage, he was ten years older, a lot bigger, and a lot stronger. Kind of a "Jungle Jim" Loscutoff type, he would back us in and simply overpower us. I learned quickly to close my mouth and clinch my jaw while trying to stop him. Many times, I would watch his shot come out the bottom of the net while sitting on the blacktop looking up.

"First one to three. No more. My out," I announce like the ship's commander. I dribble the ball and start to turn so that my back is to him. I dribble with my right hand while using my left hand to provide clearance. Eamon is trying to hold me, but my weight is too much. Under the hoop I jump up and try to use the backboard to ease the ball in. Once — miss, twice — miss, three times and IN. Each time the ball came down, I managed to back him off with my body and grab the rebound.

I know I can't let him get the ball, and my energy supply is on low. I am out about twelve feet — I used to have a good jump shot on our court when I was in my mid-teens. It's not wise, but I'm desperate and shoot. The ball is a bit short, but miraculously bounces high off the front of the rim. Grabbing the rebound, I nearly bowl my nephew over as I hit a short jumper from about seven feet.

He desperately wants the ball, and images of Michael Jordan are swirling in my brain. "Control the panic!" I think. And then, "Remember how Colin did it." I back the ball in like a truck driver backing a load of beer into a firehouse to a bunch of parched firefighters who have just put out a big fire. He stabs at the ball with one hand and then the other, just missing. I can feel the hoop right behind me. I twist and lift my two hundred pound body one more time. Nothing behind me now as the ball rises seven or eight feet above the rim, and then drops silently through the basket.

Eamon has picked himself up and is walking toward the house, his head down and his left hand rubbing his neck and right shoulder. "Oh, my God," I think to myself, "he's re-injured his broken collarbone." I look back at my brother who is caught between two worlds. "Is Eamon all right?" I ask.

"Oh yeah," he says, picking up the basketball, "he'll be okay."

"No more for me," I say, "time to retire."

On this warm early-spring night, John and I stand on his home court talking quietly. Talking takes away the present uneasiness, recreates a balance. Reminiscing and connecting. The equilibrium slides back in.

"Catch a little of the game," John says.

"Sounds good to me," I say as we head to the kitchen door.

When we arrive in the family room, the Bulls are already eleven points ahead of the Knicks. Eamon is pleased. And tonight I am too.

My Life in the Theater

Up until late January of 2020, my life on the stage, with one exception, had pretty much been limited to a song sung at a variety show or the dramatic reading of a story. But starting in January, I would begin a year that saw me take to the stage for three productions, two for real and one virtual: "The Claw," "People v Carson Conners," and "Anne of Green Gables Murders Everyone." But before taking a look at each of those three productions, I would like to give some attention to a short play composed of two scenes that I had written for the faculty contribution to the student variety show at Notre Dame-Bishop Gibbons in the mid-eighties. All parts were played by the faculty — I was in the play too, as the student who forgot to do his homework in the precise way it was supposed to be done.

"THOSE DAYS"

We hear the voice of Barbara Streisand singing "The Way We Were." As the music fades, the curtain opens to a 1950's classroom scene — desks in rows, classroom neatly arranged, meticulous notes about homework past and future on the board. Students, dressed in blue blazers, grey slacks or skirts, and white shirts are sitting straight up at their desks and their book, notebook, and completed assignment rest on the right side of their desks. At the front of the teacher's desk are three brilliant apples. The teacher, a middle-aged nun, in full regalia, enters confidently from the left.

STUDENTS: *(Rising together and speaking together)* Good Morning, Sister Madeline of the Sacred Cross.

SISTER M: *(Smiling)* Good morning, Class. Please take your seats. *(Class sits down and total attention is on Sister)* Prayer, please. *(The Class joins right in as Sister begins)* 'God, grant me the serenity to accept the things I cannot change, Courage to change the things I can and the Wisdom to know the difference.' Thank you. And now let's take a look at last night's assignment. *(Students take out the assignment and place it neatly in the center of their desks as Sister walks up and down the aisles looking and nodding. She stops at the desk of a student scrunched over his paper as if to protect it. Sister slides the paper out from under his arm.)* Class, attention. Johnny seems to have forgotten one of my cardinal rules. Class, look at this paper which I am holding and tell Johnny what is wrong.

STUDENTS: *(In unison)* Johnny folded his paper.

SISTER M: Very good, Class. Now, Johnny, for your punishment, you must come every day this week after school and clap the erasers.

JOHNNY: Yes, Sister.

SISTER M: *(Now back in the front of the room)* Fine, now Class, pass the homework forward, except for Johnny who will redo on another piece of paper tonight and hand in to-morrow. *(Homework is passed up orderly)* Class, open your poetry book to page 7. Today we will read and discuss the poem "Trees" by Joyce Kilmer, a great classic that each of you will memorize for tomorrow. *(Class opens books)* Now let's all read his poem together. *(Sister notices a hand up)* Yes, Bernadette?

BERNADETTE: *(Stands at her desk)* Sister, isn't the poet a woman?

SISTER M: Why do you say that, Bernadette?

BERNADETTE: Her name is Joyce.

SISTER M: Very good, Bernadette. His full name was actually Alfred Joyce Kilmer. Alfred was a tribute to the curate, Alfred Taylor, and Joyce was an acknowledgement of Rev. Elisha Brooks Joyce, the rector of the Church the Kilmers attended. For some reason he chose the second name.

BERNADETTE: Thank you, Sister. *(She sits down)*

SISTER M: Let's read, Class. Together now.

"Trees" by Joyce Kilmer

I think that I shall never see
A poem lovely as a tree.

A tree whose hungry mouth is pressed
Against the earth's sweet-flowing breast;

A tree that looks at God all day,
And lifts her leafy arms to pray;

A tree that may in summer wear
A nest of robbins in her hair;

Upon whose bosom snow has lain;
Who intimately lives with rain.

Poems are made by fools like me,
But only God can make a tree.

SISTER M: Ahhhhhh. What an absolutely lovely poem. Would anyone like to say anything about Mr. Kilmer's masterpiece?

STEVEN: *(Standing)* I was wondering, Sister, why would Mr. Kilmer call himself a fool.

SISTER M: Very good, Steven. If you look carefully, you will notice that Mr. Kilmer is making a comparison. Do you see with whom?

STEVEN: Hummmm, God?

SISTER M: Exactly. Now, what did God create in the poem?

STEVEN: The tree. Trees. Is he kind of saying that maybe his poem isn't equal to the creation of God's.

SISTER M: Could be, Steven. Next to God's work, the work of men pales.

STEVEN: Thank you, Sister *(Sits)*

SISTER M: Anyone else? *(Sees a hand)* Yes, Martha?

MARTHA: *(Standing)* The nest of robbins in her hair? Can you explain?

SISTER M: Sure. You know, sometimes you wear a pretty jewel in your hair and it enhances your beauty. Kilmer might be saying that the nest of robbins enhances the beauty of the tree, and even shows in the unity of God's creation that it welcomes the birds.

DWIGHT: *(Blurts out)* I don't understand that.

SISTER M: Dwight, you know the rules of the class. You never shout out or even say something without raising your hand.

DWIGHT: *(Hangs head)* Yes, Sister, I'm sorry.

SISTER M: Dwight, today be here at 3 sharp, and we will have a further chat about manners.

DWIGHT: Yes, Sister. I'm sorry.

SISTER M: Thank you, Dwight. Now class, can anyone give me an example of one technique the poet employs in "Trees." *(Sister looks around and sees a hand raised.)* Yes, Ellen.

ELLEN: *(Standing)* In stanza three, Kilmer uses the words "looks," "lifts," and "leafy." That's called alliteration.

SISTER M: Wonderful, Ellen, and since you are standing, would you be able to tell the class what you call two poetic lines that rhyme?

ELLEN: Couplets, and *(she looks at poem)* the poet had six sets of couplets in this poem.

SISTER M: Excellent, Ellen. Please be seated. Class, time is almost up for today. For tonight, you will memorize Joyce Kilmer's "Trees" and be ready to come up to the front of the room and recite the poem by heart. You can practice in front of your parents.

CLASS: Yes, Sister.

Lights Fade Out and Curtain.

"THESE DAYS"

Pink Floyd's "The Wall" is blasting away and begins to fade as the curtain opens to a 1980's classroom. Desks are in disarray with students scattered about, a number slouched in their desks, a couple of students are sitting across their desks. Students are dressed in jeans and tee shirts, boots and sneakers many with laces loose. The teacher, Sister Lucy, a woman in her thirties, wearing a beige skirt and a white shirt with a small cross on her collar enters the room. She heads toward a desk that appears to be in some order, unlike the rest of the room. No one is paying attention.

SISTER LUCY: Class, Class! Sit down and sit up, if that makes any sense.

CLASS: Sure, Sister, whatever you say. (*They settle into their seats.*)

SISTER LUCY: Prayer, please. Dear Lord, help us all in this time of need. Ok, please take out the homework.

BOB: What homework?

MARIE: I didn't have my book. Couldn't do it.

DAVE: (*Looking through papers*) Not sure, what was the homework?

SISTER LUCY: (*Fingers running through her hair*) I asked you to show what Joyce Kilmer's attitude toward trees was in about a hundred words, and give me a few lines from the poem to back your thought up.

CARRIE: Nuts, I think I read a poem called "Stumps."

SISTER LUCY: Ok, QUIET! Could I get a volunteer to read their paragraph?

MARK: Sister, was Joyce a fag? (*Laughs and grunts*)

SISTER LUCY: Mark, he uses the last name of a minister who had a major influence in his life. The name does not mean that he is gay, and besides, you guys, one's sex doesn't determine if one can write a poem or not. *(Student walks in and flops into a seat in the back row)* Dave, you're late. Detention for you.

DAVE: Come on, Sister, give me a break. I was in the bathroom. Can't a guy have a good visit around here? Is this a prison?

SISTER LUCY: See me after class. Now, let's get back to the poem. Let's try reading it together again. *(She starts, but few join in except for mumbling.)*

BARB: Sister, really, can't we read something good, you know, like "The Night the Dopes Came Over," by Steve Martin, you know the SNL guy.

SISTER LUCY: No, *(hands to her forehead)* we are discussing "Trees."

DUKE: Ok, this is legit — a question — What about all these references to sex — I mean bosoms and breasts — kind of risky.

SISTER LUCY: You mean risqué. To answer your question, let's go back and look at the start of the poem.

DICK: That's stupid - lovely as a tree. Who cares?

GLORIA: Did this guy use drugs or anything? Could he be tripping?

BILL: *(Excited)* You're right. Look! He sees a tree whose mouth is sucking the ground. And he's got his arms out all day - probably looking for a hit.

NANCY: *(Sitting up)* Yes!! The guy is on Cocaine — there's snow in his tree. *(The whole class is now completely alert and buzzing and as Sister Lucy hangs her head, Nancy stands and starts reciting with vigor and enthusiasm the poem, and now the whole class is standing and speaking louder and louder, almost shouting and the final lines rings out —*

"Poems are made by FOOLS like ME
But only GOD can make a TREE."

And the Shows Went On

One Sunday morning at our Church in the late spring of 2019, a group of us (we had grown into a little community within the larger) were chatting before Mass began when Phyllis — a member with me of the Curriculum Committee of Union College Academy for Lifelong Learning (UCALL) — approached me and told me about a project she was working on. She had been translating for some time from Polish to English a manuscript of a play by Zygmunt Brzozowski entitled *Pazura (The Claw)*. The manuscript had been found a number of years earlier in the attic of her mother's girlhood home, when the property was being prepared for sale. The typed manuscript had been mimeographed in the familiar blue font, and was now faded on fragile yellowed paper.

What made Phyllis's work especially exciting was that she had known the playwright when she was growing up — a family friend, who had been in her parents' wedding. Brzozowksi had also been an active member of a theater organization known as the Maska Dramatic Circle, which had been formed in Schenectady in 1933 and "had performed more than 51 plays in Polish for appreciative audiences until 1942." Phyllis had written a history of this group.

In her research about the play itself, she found very little except in a local historical document that indicated *Pazura* was performed on Sunday, May 14, 1939, perhaps the one and only time. Phyllis notes, "My father, Stanley Zych, played the lawyer Syska, and my mother, Sophie Korycinski, played one of the potential heiresses, Klara Makowka."

In her research, Phyllis discovered that *The Claw* was an adaptation of a 1922 stage play by John Willard called *The Cat and the Canary*. It had been adapted at least four times into feature films, the most famous a 1939 film starring Bob Hope.

She had felt obligated "to translate this precious document." Now, nearing the end of that major task, Phyllis's mind had leapt to the idea of doing a dramatic reading of the play, employing members of UCALL. As Co-Chair of the UCALL Winter Committee Program, Phyllis had suggested to her committee that she might be able to have the play as part of the winter program. Now, she was starting to take action: Might I be interested in being part of this production of a comic murder mystery?

I told Phyllis I might be and that helped to get things rolling. She began in earnest to gather volunteers mostly from UCALL and within a few weeks we gathered for the first time at Phyllis's house with only one experienced Thespian in the group. The one exception was Rob Weinzimer, the brother of a member of the Winter committee, Stella Collins. Rob had had some acting lessons and had performed in a number of plays in his home state of Maryland. For all our rehearsals, except the one before the actual performance, Rob would join us via phone.

The rehearsals, usually starting at one and running three hours, were in an ideal setting — Phyllis's kitchen. She had soda and water, nuts, chips, pretzels, and even an assortment of candies. Once we got rolling, cast members would bring treats, and Bonnie always brought her six pack of Coke, which she willingly shared with others.

What was the play about? Here is a description taken from the May 9, 1939 *Gazette.* "The plot of the play centers on a will left by an eccentric old man who had made a fortune here in America and had no one to whom to leave his estate. So he made a most extraordinary will that becomes a bone of contention among his distant relations. The person who finally inherits the fortune of Horacyjusz Burak also inherits a pack of trouble because she arouses the ill will of the other claimants. Zosia Burak, a very distant relative of the old man, becomes the target of a murder plot and various other unpleasant surprises. The play is fast moving and packed with action."

Our first reading as a group was as expected a bit rough as we tried to get a grip on our characters as well as the dynamic with others. The other factor that produced both amusing and exasperating moments was our pronunciation of certain character names in the play that were in Polish. The character Stas Chmurka's last name is pronounced as "h" as in "hmmmmoorka," which often came out with the Ch sound. With the character Broncia Cukierek, the "cia" is pronounced as ch in church; "cu" is pronounced as ts: Broncha Tsookerek. Phyllis was patient with us for a while, and then began to get more severe until we got it down.

I played Paul Polonowicz, a potential heir, and also a former and still admirer of Zosia Burak (potential heir played by Phyllis Budka, our translator of the text and organizer of this production), whom we discover by the end of the first act is named as the one who inherits the fortune, much to the chagrin of the other guests who were possibilities. One factor that complicates my character's life is that I have a dark history with another character by the name of Tomasz Pasternack (played by Art Clayman), who also has a history with Zosia, thus a conflict with my character. By the end of the first act, Marek Syska (played by Jim Comly, a UCALL committee member who was not interested in being in the play until he was told that his character would be dead by the end of act 1), the lawyer who is in charge of the reading of the will, has disappeared, and the suspense has begun to build, especially after the sudden arrival of an asylum guard, Grzegorz Kapusciak (played by Rob Weinzimer). Kapusciak speaks to us of the escape from a prison of a particularly dangerous inmate, who may be on the prowl in the neighborhood. During the first act, the long-time servant of the house, the mysterious Kunnegunda Pirog (played by another friend of Phyllis's — Elizabeth Paul) has added enough touches - allusions to ghosts, secrets of the house, and strange voices — to build a scary comic tension.

I had read only the first act of *The Claw* ahead of time — even though I told Phyllis I had read through the entire play. Life seemed to be extremely busy at the time, and I figured I would discover more about my character in the group reading. So far he seemed a bit murky to me — undisclosed past tensions with Tomasz, some obscure romantic history with Zosia, a tendency to be brusque and quick tempered — I hoped Act 2 would flesh him out more.

Act 2 rachets up the tension as Zosia, trying to be fearless and strong, gives in to panic and fear. Before she is hammered with the hardest truth, she engages in conversation with Kunnegunda who points out that the bed Zosia will sleep in is the same bed in which Uncle Horace, the creator of the will, died. The plot thickens with dramatic loud knocks, infighting between two of the guests — Clara and Broncia, Tomek and Paul once again attempting to win Zosia over and both vowing to protect Zosia against whatever threat emerges, and Stas complicating matters by making his case to woo Zosia, as they share memories of their childhood together. The action intensifies further with a foreboding letter written by the late Uncle Horace, the discovery of a secret panel, and a necklace, and then as Zosia tries to sleep, the appearance of a Claw thrust from the panel, the claw touching Zosia's throat — and then her screams, everyone running to see what has happened and Act 2 climaxing as the panel is opened and all — horror struck — see the body of Marek Syska — dead.

Well as we paused for a short break, it was clear that the dangers were real — we had a dead body in front of us. One short act to go, and I wondered what role my character would have in the resolution of this play. Who would emerge heroic? Who would be the villains? And we returned.

Act 3 is marked with fear, confusion, panic, and a touch of humor as we work toward the end. Low and behold I am the villain in cahoots with the asylum guard Kapusciak. And my motive — I felt I was the rightful heir. I scream at Zosia, "You lied and stole my inheritance from me. I was supposed to be his heir." And then to be true to the old cliche that there is no honor among villains, Kapusciak and I begin a verbal and then physical battle over a gun Kapusciak has been holding. The gun flies to the floor as Tomek and Stas rush in to the rescue. Zosia picks up the gun and hands it to Tomek. As order is restored, Tomek leads the two criminals out to the police. Stas makes his final plea to Zosia that after all of this she might consider him as a husband. The audience is smiling as the play ends with Zosia who has been struggling all along with Stas's half-baked ideas saying, "Oh, Stasiu, at last you have a good idea... right? Kiss me, my dear."

And so we had begun, the first reading over. Rehearsals followed during the fall, once a week if we could manage it. About the third week of rehearsals, we realized that the sound effects we were trying to make with our own voices and pots and pans banged on by our narrator Gail needed to have a professional touch. So we reached out to UCALL veteran and skilled technician Bob Saltzman and asked him if he could join us for rehearsals and establish when a visual or sound effect might work. Bob was gracious and generous with his time and usually sat in during the rehearsals listening to us do the readings and then offering his ideas about what might work to enhance the production.

But now the plot thickens — for me!

One day well into our fall rehearsal period, Bonnie McCullough, who was playing potential heiress Klara Makowka, pulled me aside during our break. "I was wondering if you could do me a favor. We just had someone drop out of our UCALL Mock Trial, and I was wondering if you might be able to fill in." I hesitated and asked her how major the part was, and she said, "You're just a witness. And we won't be having rehearsals — I'll give you a script and just get down the basics for your character." That was a relief, more rehearsals would have been too much, so I said that I would do it. She would bring the script to our next rehearsal, which she did. I didn't pay too much attention to it for a week or so, and then one day picked it up off my desk. I sent her an email and asked her again who my character was. She said, "Carson Conners."

The case was "People v. Carson Conners," a case used a few years prior in the New York State Mock Trial Tournament. My name as the central focus of the case did not bode well for my small role. Then I took a look at the case and my character.

In "People v. Carson Conners," I was a witness all right but also the defendant! I was a nineteen year old high school student on trial trying to defend myself against a disorderly conduct charge: if found guilty, I would serve a term of imprisonment not exceeding fifteen days and a fine not exceeding two hundred and fifty dollars.

This legal treatment of a student was part of the school's "zero-tolerance" policy, which fit right into the bypassing of traditional school discipline in what had become known as a "school-to-prison pipeline." The heart of my so-called guilty action was refusing a teacher's direction in the hallway to report to the assistant principal's office after the teacher, Lauren Smith, had observed what she considered my inappropriate behavior with another student. When I refused to respond to her direction, she grabbed my arm to try to direct me to the office. It is then that I yelled at her to "Take your damn hands off me. You can't tell me what to do you freakin' idiot. Go screw yourself."

These words by Carson told me two things: having taught forty seven years at Notre Dame-Bishop Gibbons, I had never had a student speak to me this way and thus such words were anathema to me and would be hard to defend; second, this role was going to be a real challenge. And so I began over the next few weeks to become very familiar with the case of Carson Connors and the school he attended: Bigtown High School in Bigtown, New York. The Casebook included a four page statement of the case itself, the affidavits of six principal characters (including Connor's) who figured in the actual case, and then appendices of assessment exam stats, the school's disciplinary policy with four pages of rules that figured into my case, city court info on my specific violent behavior, and the supporting deposition signed by Lauren Smith (teacher) and Bobbie Jones (School Resource Officer).

Now well into fall, I had two characters to become more familiar with and to fine-tune. Paul Polonowicz, the vengeful killer in *The Claw*, became more and more fun as our group would gather and spend as much time laughing as we did working on our characters: I particularly enjoyed jousting with Tomek Pasternak because Art was getting into his character as much as I was. I needed to work a bit more on how dastardly I was in the final scene after I had been exposed as the killer. Carson Connors was more nerve-wracking, in some ways a bigger challenge. I studied the case carefully and then called on the assistance of my wife, who is an attorney, to help me with what a witness should and shouldn't do in responding to an attorney's questions. I followed her words of wisdom with a visit to ND-BG and a chat with one of the outstanding coaches of our superb mock trial team, Linda Neidl. ND-BG had won an inordinate number of county championships in mock trial and been to the State Finals a few times. Linda, the chair of the English Department, had some advice and then she gave me a document that proved to be quite helpful.

First of all, the essence of Debbie's advice was to focus on the question and answer just the question. I have a tendency to ramble and to digress. That she said would be dangerous. She was also able to apply her advice with me when I obtained a document related to the trial from Linda. Notre Dame-Bishop Gibbons had dealt with this exact case two years prior in the State Mock Trial competition. Linda still had on file the direct and cross of Carson Connors that the team had used in preparation for the competitions. I felt as If I had discovered gold. With these questions, Debbie was able at home to not only question me from the defense and prosecution but also signal me when enough was enough. After a few run-throughs, I began to get a pretty good feel for the case and my role. I felt that I would play Carson as unfairly treated and judged and though my verbal outburst was somewhat extreme, I would contend that I had "lost it" and felt contrite over that.

Back at *The Claw*, we were growing into a pretty smooth-running team — the UCALL Players we named ourselves — and Bob Saltzman had elevated our production with appropriate sounds and visual effects that would appear behind us on a screen during the production, which now — thanks to Phyllis's efforts with Union College's Theater chair Randy Wyatt — would be staged at Yulman Theater on the Campus of Union. We had rehearsal set for January 27th, dress rehearsal for January 29th and the show at 1 p.m. on January 30th.

The Mock Trail was set for January 28th at 1 p.m. in the Nott Memorial Chapel on the campus of Union College. The Judge for the case would be Deborah Slezak, Esq. a partner at Cioffi-Sleazak-Wildegrube, P.C. The Prosecution would be Joseph Sise, Esq. and the Defense Robert Abdella, Esq. The two gentlemen were partners in the law firm of Abdella and Sise, personal injury attorneys. Before joining this firm, Joe Sise had been Supreme Court Judge for twenty years. What made this occasion a bit unnerving for me was the fact that I had taught three of his children at Notre Dame-Bishop Gibbons, all excellent students and had known him in that context. I had actually attended a few of the mock trials that his children were in for our high school.

The mock trial participants met on a weekday morning a few days before the trial to clarify the structure and plan for the trial.

In Memorial Chapel the audience of about 130 or so people were read the following statement by UCALL Moderator Bonnie McCullough: "Welcome to the trial of Carson Conners, a high school student accused of disorderly conduct for aggression against a fellow student. Sound simple? Perhaps, but as you observe this trial play out, you might find yourself questioning whether your verdict will be guilty or not guilty. Following the trial and during the break, use the ballot you have to register your vote."

The three witnesses for the prosecution and the three for the defense were all played by UCALL members. I sat at a table on the stage next to my defense attorney. I had worn kakis, a light blue shirt, and a cardigan sweater, in my attempt to portray a low-key, conservative student who was a decent kid who had briefly lost his cool.

I recall vividly a few moments from the trial: the first happened at the start of the trial when Judge Sise (I thought of him as the judge he had been) — tall, stately, and handsome — addressed the jury, the audience, and with his left arm gestured in my direction. What I recall is not verbatim, but in my mind, it captures the essence of what he was saying. "Look at this guy and consider this: his teacher after observing what she considered inappropriate behavior in the hallway — pushing another student — asked him to come with her to the assistant principal's office. What would most students have done? We all know. This guy, however, stepped back and screamed at her — listen to these words — "Take your damn hands off me. You can't tell me what do do you freakin' idiot. Go screw yourself." He paused as the entire audience stared at me. "Is this the type of student we want walking the halls of our high schools?" He turned back to the jury. "Today's case will show clearly that Carson Connors is guilty as charged of Disorderly Conduct and should receive the appropriate punishment." I must admit that I felt reduced to a slug, but another part of me was ready to fight for Connor in a system that appeared to be loaded against students who don't fit the image of the good student. The truth is we are not the losers they say we are.

Another moment that rings out is part of my personal defense — I had said that the teacher grabbed me by the arm, whereas the teacher had said she touched my arm to indicate direction. In responding to both Judge Sise and to my defense attorney, I had used my left hand to very forcefully grab my right arm to show how the teacher had grabbed me thus suggesting how my verbal outburst was more instinctive than malicious, followed with the line, "I know I shouldn't have said what I did, but her accusation of me doing something wrong when I hadn't done anything wrong triggered my reaction." As I recall, Judge Sise tried to keep my wording to a minimum at this moment.

My hope leaped up at one moment during my attorney's questioning of Lauren Smith, the teacher, played by UCALL member Stella Collins. If I remember correctly, she recalled a moment following the incident that was inconsistent with her affidavit. In the affidavit, she had said that both security guards had rushed to the scene of the incident, but in her testimony, she indicated that only Bobbie, the one guard, was there. Whatever the precise inconsistency was, it was enough to create a bit of doubt.

I think the final factor in the trial was that there appeared to be on the part of school officials an effort to get mediocre students out of the way at assessment time to avoid the school and particular teachers — Miss Smith was one — from looking bad. My suspension pending trial was enough to keep me from taking the assessment test, suggesting that the school's action was an example of an institution gaming the system.

After the break, the Judge was given the results of the Jury's balloting. Following a few preliminary words, she announced the ruling — "Not Guilty." Such sweet sounds, such relief!

The Claw was close — two days away, but now my life was much more in balance. The judgment of "Not Guilty" had tipped the scales back to even — I knew that what was coming was a guilty culprit being led out of the old estate with a gun in my back held by my old rival Tomek Pasternak.

The rehearsal had gone well, and the day of the show was cold, but clear. We all dressed in black with our one individualizing characteristic, a hat of our own choosing. We had a pretty good audience of maybe a hundred or more, and we sat in a semicircle on the floor in front of them.

After Phyllis's introduction, we were off, and enhanced by some excellent special effects and visuals by Bob we read well, the dialogue flowing smoothly from one character to the next. Phyllis had asked me for a picture that she could give Bob for his visuals, and the most dramatic moment came when I was about to be exposed — Bob had a mean-looking wolf on the screen behind us and at the moment when I emerge out of the darkness in the last scene and Zosia, now realizing who the criminal is, screams out "Paul," the screen changes from the wolf to my peaceful look on the deck at Raquette Lake. Then to my utter surprise, Kunnegunda, seated to my immediate right, reaches over and rips the hat off my head. It made sense when I thought of it later, but at the moment I thought, "Why is this woman attacking me?"

As the audience began their applause, we all stood and bowed together. Then there was music and roses for Phyllis, and *The Claw* had come to an end, except for our little cast gathering a week later where I read a poem I had written.

THE CLAW AND THE UCALL PLAYERS

Fantastyczny (Fon Tas STICH NEE)
The crowd was roaring — My God, we did it,
she thought, as the polka music played on.
"Come on, Jim, get down here with us —
you're not Siska any longer —
Ah that's it, yup, come on up and bow with us."
Her arms filled with flowers
and the audience raved on.

She looked left and right —
Rob, Art, Paul, Elizabeth, now Jim, David
and then Betty Carol, Bonnie, and Gail
and oh yes — BOB! the master
of the audio and visuals.
It had been a long road
that began in her mind a year ago
And that she shared with a friend in Church
one Sunday morning.
She had done the translation
But now —-
What would it take, she mused.
A committed cast willing to put in the time
And casting — could she get the right people?
Hummmmmm — Who to play Stas, the hero,
who rises from "On one hand" or "On the other hand"
to send for the priest so that he can ask
for Zosia's hand in marriage?
Or who to play the garrulous heiress
Broncia Cukierek?
Or the mysterious and remote Kunnegunda?
Or the sarcastic and sardonic Tomek?
And then all the pieces began to fall into place
And each person seemed to fit the part.
Oh, there were frustrations
with projection — "Speak UP!"
And how many times did she have to scream
There is NO C in CHMURKA!!
Gail on pots and pans
was not enough
She needed someone who could put flesh on the bones —

that vital dimension of sound and visual.
She knew who could do it —
But with his commitments and schedule
would this send him over the edge?
And then he said YES.
And Boy did he do it —arriving with a plethora
of ideas about making the play sing.
And then the venue — maybe?
Valerie and Randy and yes!!
We had it — Yulman Theater.
And the date was set!
The audio and visual crew were ready
The cast members were psyched
And the audience watched the UCALL PLAYERS
perform with gusto and style Zygmont Brzozowski's"
"The Claw."
And Physllis was very, very happy.
Bravo! Bravo! Bravo!

We tried to bring our UCALL Players back to put on a performance of Orson Welles "The War of the Worlds," but COVID was moving in and getting stronger and even though we looked at simple old radio shows and one-act plays as simpler possibilties, there were too many forces arrayed against us. And we withdrew into our fortresses to fend off COVID.

Months passed…

And then the phone rang again — it was Phyllis. She had an offer. Randy Wyatt had written a literary comedy horror in one act called "Anne of Green Gables Murders Everyone," and he was looking for a few UCALL Players. In fact his theater class was collaborating with students from Northern Hills Middle School in Grand Rapids, Michigan, who were under the guidance of teacher and director of theater Amisha Groce. This production would integrate members of the UCALL PLAYERS, students from Union College, and middle-school students from Northern Hills.

Now before I move ahead, I must confess that there are gaps in my reading that stun some people. Some of my more academic friends have shown some disbelief when I admit that I have not read *War and Peace* and *Middlemarch* — to choose two classics that one might assume English majors and teachers of English for forty-seven years might have read. Still, the reaction does not compare to the shock when I admit that I have not read *Winnie-the-Pooh* or *The House at Pooh Corner.* "Oh, my goodness, are you serious?" And then the ones with the sharper digs, "Really, how could you be a teacher of English all these years and not have read Winnie?" Announcing that you have read Dante's *Inferno* more than thirty times does not save you from a verbal lashing. Now, I have to admit and only Debbie knows this, I had never read L. M. Montgomery's *Anne of Green Gables* nor had I seen what I have heard is the most famous of the film adaptations, the 1985 production, with Colleen Dewhurst and Richard Farnsworth. With obligations and commitments pressing hard, I chose to have Debbie give me a quick idea of the story and then read two plot summaries. As the two nights approached for the presentation of the play, I was struggling to find the best voice and stance for Matthew Cuthbert and did a dangerous thing — I looked at a few scenes featuring Richard Farnsworth in the movie. I didn't want to emulate him, but I wanted a bit more feel of the character.

I must admit that of the fifteen or so characters, my character of Matthew and Phyllis Butka's character of Matthew's sister Marilla were major figures right behind the young woman playing the lead of Anne Shirley, performed by a

Union College student Sophie Hurwitz. Marilla and Matthew are an elderly brother and sister who have decided to adopt a boy from an orphanage to help with chores on their farm. They get Anne by mistake.

On the first few reads, Union's Theater director guided us and then Amisha Groce stepped in for the last few rehearsals.

The play is bananas, crazy. Once Anne enters the scene, she dominates — verbal, opinionated, hyperbolic, and dangerous, especially if anyone makes a reference to her red hair. Though Marilla is initially set on not accepting her, Matthew finds her strangely appealing. It is clear that Marilla tends to dominate Matthew, but he sees in Anne possible relief, a friend, someone to cut into the drab routine of his life.

As a decision is being made about Anne's future, she is quietly dispatching people — neighbors and busybodies who make disparaging comments about her — by choking them with her red braids or slipping poison into their tea. She hides their bodies under rugs and carries with her a suitcase that emits disturbing sounds.

It is clear that at Green Gables Anne is on a mission to alter the world and Matthew is being drawn to Anne's vision. Anne casts a spell on a young neighbor Diana with whom she exchanges a lock of hair and then seals their pact by drinking a purple drink leading Diana to say, "Ooo. Raspberry cordial!"

Matthew finds on the table a text which explains everything about the Avonlea Prophecy, regarding the future of their town of Avonlea. The heart of the prophecy is that an Outsider will come and change their world. More die as they consume a cake made by Anne. Matthew says to Anne, "Your cake was …a sensation."

In scene 5, Matthew and Anne speak of what has happened. Matthew says, "Before you came, there was nothing.

Nothing happened. All the same. Drudgery." He goes on, "Your imagination. Your view of the world. Your sense of ... purpose. I am in awe of your sense of purpose. I wonder. Do you know your purpose?" And Anne responds, "My purpose is to destroy this world so a New One can come about." And with that Matthew says, "Only one thing to be done. Let's get you to school."

With the school becoming infected by Anne's power, she faces another challenge when Gilbert, a dashing young student, approaches Anne after realizing that she is the Outsider. After an initial coming together — both praising each other — Gilbert makes a reference to her hair, "like carrots." With that Anne shatters a slate over his head, and Gilbert is dispatched to the nether world.

The play ends with Matthew and Anne sitting at the edge of the island in the moonlight. As Matthew speaks of Anne being his "Soulful love," Anne takes off her wig and puts it on Matthew. Matthew then tells her that Marilla was arrested after poisoning the cheesemonger, which leads Anne to say, "Filthy murderer," and Matthew to respond, "You think you know someone."

Anne will soon have all in Avonlea under her command, and Matthew sees that she has more purpose than anyone in Avonlea. Matthew acknowledges that he is not long for this world: a heart attack awaits after he experiences a financial failure — capitalism. Friend Diana shows up with her dog Lyndey and Matthew speaks of "Soulful friends." The play closes with the dog barking, "Ruff," and Matthew responding,"Yes, the water is rough tonight." Anne in one of her classic poetic hyperboles says, "The water is like a hundred thousand obsidian gemstones," to which Matthew says, "Stunning," and Diana, "Exquisite." The closing line is Anne's, "The world, in its last breath, will be a marvel."

On February 26th and 27th at 7 p.m., the Union College Theater Department presented via Zoom "Anne of Green Gables Murders Everyone." I had my scariest moment with the production on the rehearsal night of the 25th. The challenge of the Zoom production was to carefully anticipate the scenes when you were on, and when you weren't to kill your sound and your video. On rehearsal night, just a few lines before I was to come back on, Casey, our beloved cat, jumped up on my desk and walked across the keyboard leaving me with a blank screen. I don't know what I touched to bring the screen back, but the Theater Gods were with me. There were only two lines left in the script before my next line. I realized it was only rehearsal, but it created a sense of panic in me, and so the night of the production I closed the door to the room so that Casey could not endanger the performance of "Anne of Green Gables Murders Everyone."

In a little over one year, I had become a killer desperate for his inheritance, a nineteen year old arrested and charged with disorderly conduct in a school, and a lonely old man who finds his soulmate in a young woman destined to change the world he lives in. Shakespeare said that "one man in his time plays many parts." So true — and I had added three characters to my repertoire.

Moments... and Onward

FROM THE PARK BENCH

Some journeys end far too soon. When you are a teacher for many years, you have those very sad moments when students you taught die. Tami Williams, Class of 2000, passed away suddenly at the age of 38. She had a life with her own sadnesses, losing two sisters. She also had a son whom she loved and cherished. We had chatted on and off over the months prior to her death, and she was excited to tell me more about the world of crystals and all she had learned. She also loved horoscopes and exploring in what sense people's signs were compatible — so human, ordinary conversations about each other's interests. A couple of years prior to her last few months, Tami and I had a chat, and that conversation is something special I will hold onto because it spoke of her humor, her imagination, and her potential.

Tami and I were seated on a bench in Stockade Park in Schenectady, which runs along the Mohawk River. She had asked me to meet her to discuss a few ideas she had percolating, one about putting together a collection of stories. It was a lovely day, and the river flowed gently by. As we sat there chatting and doing a lot of laughing, a canoe appeared on the river to our left. In it were two people: a woman in the front and a man in the back.

"What do you think?" Tammy asked.

"What do you mean?" I responded.

"Well," she sighed as if to get me caught up, "What's the relationship? husband and wife? People on a date? Just friends?"

"I don't know," I said and looked more carefully at the couple. The woman, maybe about thirty and in good shape, seemed to be paddling with more vigor than the slightly overweight man who sat in an almost relaxed way in the back of the canoe. "Maybe friends, but not too close — energetic woman and lazy man."

She laughed, "Nah, I think they've been going out for a while, kind of set in their ways, but she's the leader — look at her go." The woman seemed to dig in harder with her paddle.

They moved out of our vision to the right, and we continued to talk about a recent painting she had been working on. The sun was easy, and the park was quiet, except for an occasional bicyclist who cruised by us.

"Look! Oh my God!" Tami was sitting on the edge of the bench pointing up to the right. "She's not there! He's alone!"

"Really?" I said calmly, gazing at the lone figure in the canoe.

"Yes! Ahhhhh!! What do you think? What happened?"

"I don't know," I said, a smile crossing my face, "maybe she had an appointment, and he just dropped her off."

She looked directly at me, "Really?" She paused, "Or maybe he killed her! And right now we are the only ones who know!"

"How do you know she isn't lying down in the canoe, and they are having fun with us?" I said, as a smile broke out on my face.

"She jumped up on the bench and stood on her tiptoes, "No, I could see her. There's nothing there!"

"Maybe she's watching us from the woods across the way," I said.

She stared at the woods for a few seconds. The man had picked up speed in the canoe and was heading for a landing area near Jumpin' Jacks.

"He's going to get away with it," she said, jumping back to the ground, and then we looked at each other, then out to the water again — maybe a floating body, and then back at each other and then laughter, you know, the kind where your whole body shakes and tears come down.

"You know what, Tami?"

"What?" she got out through her laughter.

"I think your first story should be about the mystery of the couple in the canoe."

She laughed again and then said, "Maybe it will be." I think at that moment we both looked out at the river and towards the direction the canoe had gone. Nothing. And the river was still.

THE MAN ON THE CROSS

On a Saturday Zoom retreat from the Campion Center near Boston, we were shown a painting to reflect on and react to in writing. Simply described, it was a crucified figure, a black man, a stark scene presented to the viewer from a low angle. The essence of the painting seemed so simple, and I saw my role in the scene.

THE MAN ON THE CROSS

The man on the Cross
Looks down
He seems to look at me
And past me
He is a black man
And he knows in his Soul
That I failed him
Yes I saw him
On the Road
And I did not reach out
Was it fear?
Was it prejudice?
Was it my inability to see
That the man with me
On the road
Was Christ, my brother
He looked at me
But I did not see.
In the lateness of today
I begin
To see.

"A MINISTER OBSERVED"

Many years ago when my brother Leo (a priest) was stationed at St. Paul the Apostle in Schenectady (his first parish), he would take Communion to parishioners who were unable to get to Mass. One was Mr. Pigliavento, a farmer, who lived on Lydius Street. Leo would sometimes walk right into the field where Mr. Pigliavento was working, and Mr. P would get down off his tractor to receive Communion. Thirty years later, my wife Debbie, as a Eucharistic Minister, would take Communion to the very same man, now an old gentleman nearly blind who sat waiting in his kitchen. I would accompany her, and I was always touched by the moment and their relationship. One Sunday afternoon after she had brought him Communion, I sat down and wrote this poem. My niece Kathryn did the calligraphy.

a minister observed

Alone in blue,
he sits fingering on his lap
    a folded paper towel.
she moves near him.
her long, tanned fingers rest on
his ancient hands. she begins,
"Heavenly Father..." and her words
form gentle waves of strength.
    Now her right hand moves with grace
    to take the host from the golden pyx.
    the old man swallows to prepare.
    dimly, he sees the whiteness
    held before him.
    "the Body of Christ." she places
    the Host on his tongue.
In this moment of Communion,
i look down.
the hands have returned, more words.
with "Amen" he raises her hands
to his lips. and then speaks, "thank you."

A MINISTER OBSERVED

Alone in blue
he sits fingering on his lap
a folded paper towel.
She moves near him.
Her long, tanned fingers rest
on his ancient hands. She begins,
"Heavenly Father…" and her words
form gentle waves of strength.
Now her right hand moves with grace
to take the host from the golden pyx.
The old man swallows to prepare.
Dimly, he sees the whiteness
held before him.
'The Body of Christ." She places
the Host on his tongue.
In this moment of Communion
I look down.
The hands have returned, more words.
With "Amen" he raises her hands
to his lips. And then speaks, "Thank you."

LOOKING BACK AND THEN ...

For us the last trip — to Boston
in early March of 2020 to see my brother —
shortly after that
the virus and the word spread
All that was normal was going —
And normal might never be normal again.
The times grew murky and the road uncertain
with fear and heartbreak and loss
— so much we didn't know.
There were lamps of hope
in the dedication and commitment
of those who cared for others
often in precarious and dangerous environments.
The phrase "Frontline workers"
took on an awesome meaning.
It was the Biblical moment and more —
"Whatever you did
for the least of my brethren.
You did for me"
And added to that
"Whatever you did for those
who were dying
you did for all of us."
And the virus continued to spread
Menacing all — like Poe's "Red Death."
Separation rose to a new level

Dear ones alone in hospital rooms
with only a cell phone held by a nurse
to convey desperate and final words of love.

We couldn't seem to get our priorities
in proper order
to forge a unified offensive.
We were divided.
Some believed in the viral devastation
and some didn't or couldn't
and wished it away or never believed it existed.

And while lungs closed down across the land
The meaning of three words
"I can't breathe"
took on even more raw power.
Nearly empty streets became charged
with righteous and raw emotion
as people marched
crying out for justice and equality
spilling over at times into destruction.
So much already had overwhelmed
and then that one knee pushed us deeper.
And smoke and fire and indignation
Dominated each day.

Where do you stand? And with whom?
Mask or no mask?
The media was at fever pitch —
charges, attacks, and assassinations
of character — once said —

were truth. It was too late to go back.
The Truth no longer seemed to matter
And it became so hard to see
any road with all the darkness.

And then the Election
and the refusal to accept
what had happened
— for weeks
charges and attacks
of improprieties and riggings
leading to double and triple vote counting
in numerous states
until
finally
we had
the Truth.
Or so
Many of us thought.
And still doubt and disbelief
in manacled minds
And the protests grew.
The day marked
for an orderly transition of power
took us brutally back down that old road
Into violence and darkness.
We were groping and gasping
And our spirits were so low.
Where was the answer?

And then we heard
one young poet speak
on a cold January day
'For there is always light,
If only we're brave enough to see it,
If only we're brave enough to be it.'

And we began finding relief
and in the wonder of science
a beam of hope
Penetrating the darkness
As the vaccinations arrived
For the most needy at first
And though hopes were tempered
with viral variations and still-remaining
uncertainties, people offered their arms
and began to dream
of being reunited with their loved ones
of being able to breathe again
of being able to sing together
of being able to pray together
of seeing justice done
And still we wondered
If we could ever fully
turn that dark corner?

Looking back
At all that had transpired
took us past T. S. Eliot's line

"Humankind cannot stand very much reality."
Reality had come like a tidal wave
that just kept building and building
We had lost so many and so much
in one year,
we had seen such raging darkness
and yet and yet
when you looked hard
the candle was still visible - that "light"
flickering in those
who never would cease
giving all they could
to others.
Those who cared
about the simple dignity
of each person.